IACOB AND IOSEP

OXFORD UNIVERSITY PRESS
LONDON   EDINBURGH   GLASGOW   NEW YORK
TORONTO   MELBOURNE   BOMBAY
HUMPHREY MILFORD
PUBLISHER TO THE UNIVERSITY

IACOB AND IOSEP

A MIDDLE ENGLISH POEM OF
THE THIRTEENTH CENTURY

EDITED BY

ARTHUR S. NAPIER

M.A., D.Litt., Litt.D., Ph.D.

FELLOW OF THE BRITISH ACADEMY
MERTON PROFESSOR OF ENGLISH LANGUAGE AND LITERATURE
IN THE UNIVERSITY OF OXFORD

OXFORD
AT THE CLARENDON PRESS
1916

PRINTED IN ENGLAND
AT THE OXFORD UNIVERSITY PRESS

CONTENTS

The FACSIMILES represent MS. Bodley 652, folios 8ᵛ and 9ʳ, containing ll. 406–459.

INTRODUCTION

§ 1. Introductory Remarks.

THE poem here printed I copied years ago with a view to publication, and had prepared the grammar and the greater part of the introduction, but an edition by W. Heuser which appeared in the *Bonner Beiträge zur Anglistik* (ed. by Trautmann), Heft xvii (1905), caused me to lay the work aside. As, however, the poem is an interesting one, and as the *Bonner Beiträge* are not very accessible, I have decided to go on with my edition.

I wish to express my most grateful thanks to my friend Miss E. M. Overend (Mrs. Lorimer) for her invaluable help in the preparation of the glossary.

§ 2. Signs and abbreviations used.

In the glossary, phonology, and accidence ... means that this particular form occurs in other instances besides those given, whilst 'etc.' in the phonology and accidence indicates that other (i.e. different) words afford further examples of the same sound or inflexion.

ôu in the glossary and accidence indicates that the combination has the sound of *ū*, not that of the diphthong.

ŏ denotes the *ŭ* sound.

ġ denotes the *dzh* sound.

Vowel length is marked in the accidence and glossary but not in the phonology.

WG. = West Germanic.

Bülbring = Bülbring, *Altenglisches Elementarbuch.*

ESt. = *Englische Studien.*

Morsbach = Morsbach, *Mittelenglische Grammatik*.

NED. = *New English Dictionary* (*The Oxford English Dictionary*).

PBB. = *Paul und Braunes Beiträge*.

§ 3. MS.

The unique text of *Jacob and Josep* is contained in MS. Bodley 652 (Summary Catalogue No. 2306). The MS. consists of three parts written by different hands in the second half of the thirteenth century in England.

(A) foll. 1–10^b. *Jacob and Josep*. The date of the hand-writing of this part seems to be soon after the middle of the thirteenth century. Sir George Warner, to whom I sent a photograph of the MS., confirms this opinion. Between foll. 6 and 7 a leaf has been cut out.

The two other parts bound up with *J. J.* are in French:

(B) fol. 11. A French translation of the *Elucidarium* of Augustodunensis, and (fol. 46^b) a letter in French from Prester John to Frederic Barbarossa.

(C) fol. 52. The French poem *Chasteau d'Amour* by Bp. Grosseteste.

§ 4. Contents.

Jacob sits in his hall and sees his sons come home from the field. Josep begs his father to be allowed to tell him a dream he has had. Jacob bids him do so, and Josep tells how he dreamt that when they were binding the sheaves, the sheaves of the others all bowed down to his, and how the sun, moon, and eleven stars fell at his feet. Jacob thinks that the dream will certainly come true, but his brethren hearing it, hate Josep as their 'full foe'. The brethren went afield to look after the cattle, and Josep remained at home. His father sends him to seek his brethren and bring him tidings as to how they fare. He goes, but cannot find them. A man meets him wandering all alone and tells him to go to Dotaym. When he comes there, his brethren say, 'Here comes the dreamer, let us kill the scoundrel.' They seize him, intending to kill him, but Ruben interposes, so they strip him of his kirtle and put him into an empty pit. Ruben goes away, he cannot stay for pity. The others remain and commence their meal; no scruples trouble them; they laugh and consider it a great joke, and are thinking of drawing him out of the pit again and killing him, when they see two rich chapmen from Galaad coming. After some bargaining they sell Josep to them.

The merchants take him to Egypt and lead him into the city, 'which was rich and strong: castles high and proud, streets wide and long, many a fair hall and many a fair bower, white as any lily, bright as any flower.' Knights and citizens bold, ladies from their bowers and maidens free came into the street to see him, and it seemed to them as though an angel had come from heaven. The tidings soon reached Putifar, and he came and bought Josep, paying 'more than they asked'.

Jacob meanwhile is sitting in the hall, and sees his sons come home with Josep's kirtle all bloody. He falls down in a swoon and tears his hoary locks; Josep's mother rends her face and her smock.

Putifar clothes Josep in fine garments and gives him to Pharaon, whose wife soon falls in love with him. One day when the King has gone to the wood to shoot with his 'bow ibent', she sends for him and asks him for his love. On his refusal, she begins to cry out, and the King presently returning, Josep is cast into prison. Here he interprets the dreams of the King's butler and baker. Then comes

Pharaon's dream of the seven fat and lean kine (but *not* of the seven ears); and the butler, remembering Josep, tells Pharaon. Josep, ' pale and lean,' is fetched and interprets the dream, adding, ' This is thy dream, Sir King, think thou thereon. Unless Christ be thy help, Egypt is lost.' The King ponders over it by day and by night, and does not know what to do : no one could advise him. ' Then spoke an old man who was wise of speech.'

[Here a leaf is missing.]

' When I think of Abraham,' proceeds the poet, ' and the shame he suffered in Egypt on account of his wife, and how he was finally driven out of the land—if a righteous man like that suffered such shame, it seems to me no game to send to Egypt.' The brethren often brought home ' this small chaff' and made much moan for want of food. Jacob therefore sent his sons—all except Benjamin—to Egypt to buy corn. Much was the bliss they saw there. A minstrel overtook them with a harp on his back. ' Whence come you, young men ?' he said, ' It seems by your asses that you wish to buy corn. I will take you to the drawbridge and the noblest of men will entertain you to-night.' He brought them to the castle and got the porter to let them in. In the hall they see Josep and fall on their knees. Questioned they tell him that they have come from Jerusalem to buy corn, and give him the names of their father and mother. Josep feasts them and has their asses loaded with wheat, and into one of the sacks he himself puts a golden cup. Early next morning they start, but ere long twelve young men, with helmet, coat of mail, and drawn sword, overtake them and lead them back to Josep, when the cup is at once found. Josep, however, merely looks at them, and shakes his head saying,

' Cursed be treachery and he who first invented it, so many a guiltless man it brings to the ground!'

Then, learning that they have another brother at home, he sends them back again under a solemn promise to return with Benjamin. Jacob laments and falls into a swoon when he hears the news, but says they must not break their word, and he allows Benjamin to go. On their arrival Josep is overjoyed and goes to his chamber to weep for joy. He thanks the Lord that the eleven stars have come to him; if he only had his father and mother, he would have the sun and the moon as well. After the feast Josep reveals himself to his brethren and again goes to his chamber to weep for joy. Then said Ruben, ' Did I not tell you that you did wrong in sinning against the child? Now we are all done for.' Josep however, returning, kisses them all, says that his dream is not yet fulfilled, and sends them to fetch his father and kindred. Jacob, on hearing that Josep is alive, casts away his crutch, takes his mantle, plaits his hair with a silken string, takes his hat, and exclaiming that now, freed from his sorrow, he feels as though he could fly like an eagle, he rides forth singing like a child. Pharaon gives Jacob castles high and wide, and rich land by the seaside. All are happy.

It will be noted that the story as here told differs from that of the Bible in several respects.

(i) Potiphar buys Joseph and gives him to Pharaoh, and it is Pharaoh's wife, not Potiphar's, who falls in love with him.

(ii) In the Bible the brethren get the corn and, Simeon being left as a hostage, return home to fetch Benjamin. They arrive a second time and it is on this second occasion that a cup is put into the sack. It is Benjamin's sack, and Joseph says he will keep him as his servant, but will allow the others to return in peace.

In *J. J.* the brethren arrive in Egypt, get the corn, and it is on this first occasion that the cup is put into one of the sacks when Benjamin is not yet there. On the second occasion, when Benjamin is there, there is no mention of a cup or sack.

(iii) When the brethren brought Jacob news that Joseph was alive, he was evidently ill, for he threw away his crutch and felt able to fly like an eagle. He rode forth singing like a child.

If we compare the narrative of *J. J.* with the history of Jacob and Joseph as told in the *Cursor Mundi* (= *C. M.*), we find certain points of resemblance. In the case of variants (ii) and (iii) the two poems agree, the cup being put into the sack on the brethren's first visit to Egypt; and when they arrive back from their second visit, they find their father ill in bed and unable to get up and walk; but when he learns that Joseph is alive, he calls for his clothes, leaps up, and cries like a young man to his sons to make haste.

In the case of (i) the transference of the lovemaking from Potiphar's wife to Pharaoh's does not occur in *C. M.*, which here agrees with the biblical narrative, and not with *J. J.*

(iv) There is another point, a non-biblical story which I believe to have been told on the lost leaf (between fol. 6ᵇ and 7), and which we find in full in the *Cursor Mundi*, ll. 4749–4792. There we learn that after Joseph had had the corn thrashed, the chaff was thrown into the Nile and was carried down the river. Jacob happened to be walking by the Nile and saw the chaff floating down. He called his sons and bade them go up the stream, as they would be sure to find corn where the chaff came from. So the brethren went to Egypt.

From l. 330 of *J. J.* (*Ofte of his smal chaf þis breþren*

brouȝten hom) it is evident that the chaff story was known to the author of *J. J.* and was probably told on the lost leaf.

In the Old French verse translations of the Bible we find similar variants from the biblical story.   In *La Bible des sept états du monde* by Geufroi de Paris we find variants (i) Pharaoh's wife, and (iv) the chaff story.[1]   Also in Herman de Valenciennes [2] we find variants (i) and (iv).

In Jehan Malkaraume [3] and in the *Traduction anonyme de la Bible entière* [4] we find variant (i) Pharaoh's wife.   No. (iv), the chaff story, is also to be found in an old French fragment in MS. Harley 3775, extracts from which were published by P. Meyer in *Romania* 36, 188 ff.   Whether variants (ii) and (iii) are contained in any of these I do not know.

It is worth noting that even single lines in *J. J.* and *C. M.* agree closely in their contents:

(i) *J. J.* 304 :
Forþ me feccheþ Iosep, þat bloc was 7 lene.

C. M. 4547 :
For lene he was, and wan þe face.

(ii) *J. J.* 351 :
' *Berewe ȝou from care oure Louerd, þat wel mai.'*
Feire fareþ þis ȝunge men bi dai 7 bi niȝt
Into Egipte lond þat hi comen riȝt.

C. M. 4804 :
' *Godd hald ouer yow his holy hand.'*

.   .   .   .

Þai heied þam fast on þair wai,
Þat vntil Egypte son com þai.

[1] Cp. Paul Meyer in his *Notice sur la Bible des sept états du monde*, Paris, 1908, p. 274.   Professor Meyer kindly called my attention to this.
[2] Cp. Bonnard, *Les Traductions de la Bible en vers français au moyen âge*, p. 15.
[3] Cp. Bonnard, p. 59.   [4] Ibid., p. 87.

(iii) *J. J.* 410:

'*Abideþ,*' hi seiden, '*þeues, abideþ, ʒe leþ inome.*'

C. M. 4901:

'*Theues,*' said þai, '*yee most abide.*'

(iv) Cp. also *J. J.* 207 ff. with *C. M.* 4353 ff.

§ 5. **Phonology**.

A. Vowels.

(1) West Germanic *ă* before nasals.

(*a*) Before final *n* and *n* + cons. (except in the case of lengthening groups) it generally appears as *a*: *wan* 26, 27; *bigan* 34; *gan* 172 ...; *man* 62 ...; *dranc* 445; *anhonge*(*d*) 266, 414, etc. (37 instances). Far less frequently is it written *o*[1]: only the following instances occur, *onswerede* 79; *wondrinde* 76; *chapmon* 164; *þonke*(*þ*) 245, 306, 475. It should be noted however that, though *man* is, with the exception of l. 164, always written with *a*, in all the six instances where it occurs in the rhyme (31, 132, 164, 169, 335, 492) it rhymes with *ǭ* from OE. *ā*, so that the *a* is possibly due to the scribe.

(*b*) Before final *m* it appears as *a* in the preterites *cam* 87, 91 ...; and *nam* 273, 399, 401. In the preposition *from* 32 ... it is always written *o*.

(*c*) Before *m* and *n* in open syllables both *a* and *o* occur indifferently, though the *a* forms slightly predominate: *grame* 3, *grome* 233; *name* 4, *nome* 383; *ssame* 326, *ssome* 229 ...; *wone* (OE. *wana*) 317, 331; *mani* 147 ... (eight times, always with *a*); etc.

(*d*) Before the lengthening groups *mb*, *nd*, *ng*, it appears as *o*: *wombe* 7; *londe* 23 ...; *song* 5 ...; etc. (over 70 instances). Only in one case is *a* written: *wrang* 132.

---

[1] The preposition *on* is always written with *o*.

(2) OE. *æ*. This regularly yields *a* : *after* 2 ... ; *nas* 19 ... ; *fader* 35 ... ; etc. An isolated exception is *heuede* (OE. *hæfde*) 240.

(3) OE. *ea*. Before *l* + cons. (other than *d*) it regularly becomes *a* : *halle* 31 ... ; *alle* 32 ... ; *falle* 46 ... ; etc. Before *ld* it yields *ǭ* : *tolde* 35 ... ; *bolde* 151, 291 ; *biholde* 152 ... ; *olde* 252 ... ; etc. The only exceptions are *elde* 31, 169, 335 (see note). Before *r* + cons. (other than *n*) it appears as *a* : *art* 204; *armes* 222 ; *harpe* 251 ... ; etc. Before the lengthening group *rn* it becomes *ē̜* : *erne* (OE. *earnian*) 342 ; *ern* (OE. *earn*) 519 ; *bern* (OE. *bearn*) 520.

(4) OE. *eo* becomes *e* : *here* 14 ... ; *heuene* 72 ... ; etc. Before *rn* it is lengthened to *ē̜* : *ʒerne* 36. An isolated exception is *urles* (OE. *eorlas*) 291, where the *u* presumably = *ü*.

(5) Early WS. *ie*, LWS. *y*, Angl. *e, æ* (umlaut of *ea*) appears as *ē̜* in *derne* 214 ; *werne* 215. It is represented by *a* in *awaried* 427 ; *halde* (EWS. *hieldan*, Angl. *hældan*) 391.

(6) ME. *u*. This is written *u* (*v*) and *o*, and the scribe is very regular in his spelling. Initially he writes *v* in both open and close syllables : *vnirude* 20 ; *vpriʒt* 44 ; *vs* 71 ... ; *vnder-* 84 ... ; *vpon* 140 ; etc. Medially he writes *o* in open syllables and *u* in close syllables (except after *w*, when he uses *o*). Instances are (*a*) in open syllables : *bote* 4 ... ; *loueden* 5 ... ; *comen* 8 ... ; *sones* 26 ... ; *inome* 93 ... ; *frome* 94 ... ; etc. But *trukede*[1] 393, 480 and also regularly *ssule(n)*, 56, 186 ... (*b*) In close syllables : *ful* 8 ... ; *þus* 13 ... ; *ʒunge* 34 ... ; *sunne* 48, 478; *burʒ* 145, 149; *hunger* 316 ... ; etc. But after *w* we find *o* : *wolle* 1 ... ; *worpen* 102 ... ; *worþ* 120 ... ; *wonder* 155 ... ; *iwonne* 477 ; etc. Note that *gonn(en)*

---

[1] Or is the *u* here long ?

where we should expect *u*, is regularly spelt with *o* : 46, 60, 261, 286.

(7) (*a*) OE. *y* (umlaut of *u*). The predominant representative is *u* (= *ü*): *gurdel* 7 ; *fullen* 11 ; *fulde*(*n*) 14, 260; *hul* 19 ; *dude* 24 ... ; *kurtel* 99 ... ; etc. (thirty-seven instances). On *tu-* (= *tü-*) from OE. *tyge*, cp. (12). Both *i* and *e* also occur, but much less frequently : *þinkeþ* 108 ; *kinne* 181 ; *sinne* 182 ; *kisse* 216 ... ; etc. (eleven instances). Instances of *e* are *meri* 5 ; *knetten* 43 ; *evel* 73 ; *pet* 95 ... (*pet* occurs eight times and is always so spelt); *begge* 130, 362 (in all thirteen instances). Of the foregoing examples the following occur in the rhymes :

(*a*) *knetten* (OE. *cnyttan*): *setten* (OE. *settan*) 43–4.

(*b*) *kisse* (OE. *cyssan*): *iwisse* (OE. *gewisse*) 216–17 ; *blisse* (OE. *bliss*): *kisse* 388–9 and 473–4.

(*c*) *dude* (OE. *dyde*): *stede* (OE. *stede*) 242–3 ; *arugge* (OE. on *hrycge*): *sigge* (OE. *secgan*) 360–1 ; *begge* (OE. *bycgan*): *-brugge* (OE. *brycge*) 362–3 ; *kinne* (OE. *cynne*): *sinne* (OE. *synne*) 181–2 ; *winne* (OE. *wynne*): *kunne* (OE. *cynne*) 531–2.

As the *u* (= *ü*) forms predominate so largely there seems little reason for doubting that they represent the pronunciation of the author, and that the rhyme words in group (*c*) originally all had *u* : *dude* : *stude* (OE. *styde*, cp. Sievers, PBB. x. 197, and xvi. 235) ; *arugge* : *sugge* (cp. Morsbach, § 109, n. 4 and § 133, n. 2); *bugge* : *-brugge* ; *kunne* : *sunne* ; *wunne* : *kunne*. The use of *e* and *i* in groups (*a*) and (*b*) is no doubt owing to rhyme need.

(*β*) OE. *y* from other sources also appears as *u* (= *ü*): *nuste* 197 ; *sullen* (OE. *syllan*, cp. Bülbring, § 304) 116, 118, 150, 379. For the umlaut of *ea* cp. (5). *Muche*(*l*) 20, 110 ... and *such* 12, 328, 371 ... are always written with *u*, but the pronunciation may have been *u*, not *ü*.

(8) OE. *ā* becomes *ǭ*: *one* 2, 4 ...; *gon* 6; *loþ* 9; *hom* 3² ...; *wo* 59 ...; etc. There are no instances of *a*.

(9) OE. *ēo* appears as *ē*: *lef* 9, 130 ...; *fě̄llen* 48, 50; *te* (OE. *tēon*) 77; etc. In three instances it is written *u* (probably = *ū*): *bihuld* 161; *vnfuld* 162; *athuld* 223. The personal pronoun, OE. *hēo*, is always written *heo*: 196, 216 ... OE. *ēow, ēower* appears as *ȝou* 3 ...; *ou* 22, 345; *ȝoure* 45 ...

(10) Early WS. *īe*, Non-WS. *ē* (umlaut of *ēa*) appears as *ē*: *ihere* 1 ...; *leue* 37; *isemed* 114 ...; *reme* 224, 231; etc. Isolated exceptions with *u* (probably = *ū*) are *ucchen* (OE. *īecan*) 7; *strupten* 101. Corresponding to OWS. *ȝīet* 'yet' (where the *īe* is of uncertain origin) we have *ȝut* 56, otherwise *ȝit*.

(11) OE. *ū* is regularly written *ou*, except when followed by *ht*; *nou* 1, 6 ...; *out* 7 ...; *oure* 11, 13 ...; *þou* 42 ...; *louten* 46; etc.; but *þuȝte* (OE. *þǔhte*) is always written with *u*: 4¹, 45, 47 ... The only other exceptions are¹: *hu* 71; *ure* 72, 384; *þu* 82, 83, 84, 212; *rum* 99; *bachuse* 259. Note that ME. *ū* lengthened from OE. *ǔ* before *nd* is, in the few cases where it occurs, always written *u*: (*i*) *funde*(*n*) 359, 421, 427; *grunde* 428. Possibly lengthening had not in this case taken place.

(12) OE. *ȳ* (umlaut of *ū*). This appears regularly as *u* (= *ū*). The instances are: *rume* 7; *luþer* 10, 180; *lutel* 11, 81, 405; *vnirude* 20; *ssrudeþ* 187; *ssrǔdde* 501; *prute* 215; *prude* 313, 508; *lute* 273. The only exceptions are *kin* 288, 289; *kyn* 287; *kuin* 284. In the last instance the scribe seems to have intended to write *kun* and to have then changed his mind and to have forgotten to underdot the *u*. This

¹ In *vs* (OE. *ūs*) 71 ... the *ū* had already become short: cp. Orm's *uss*.

seems to be more likely than that the *ui* is here an isolated spelling denoting *ū̆*. In *tubrugge* 363 the first *u* (= *ū̆*) has arisen from OE. *yg* (OE. **tygebrycg*).

(13) Note the influence of the *w* in *twolf* 407, 532; *wôder* 77; *forswolewed* 288; *wôlle* 1 ...

B. CONSONANTS.

(1) Initial *f* is generally written *f*, but in four instances the Southern *v* occurs: *vader* 39; *vrom* 113; *valleþ* 375; *vingres* 391.

(2) OE. *sc* is regularly written *ss*: *sseues* 43, 45; ... *ssulen* 56; ... *ssroud* 187; *Of fiss* 7 *of flesse* 503; etc.

(3) Final *n* is dropped before a consonant in *el(l)eue* 50, 476 (besides *elleuene* 471); *owe* 195; *seue* 284 ...; *o* 94, 103.

(4) After *t* an initial *þ* becomes *t*: *tis* 20; *tou* 38; *te* 48; etc.

(5) Initial *wh* has become *w*: *wat* 54 ...; *wer* 70 ...; *wen* 270 ...; *wite* 391; etc. *wh* is less common: *while* 5; etc.

§ 6. Tense formation of strong verbs.[1]

CLASS I.

Inf.[2]	Pret. Sg.	Pret. Pl.	Past Partic.
rīden	*rǭd*	—	—
—	*ouerstei3*	—	—
—	—	*rēpen*	—

---

[1] References to the instances will be found in the glossary.

[2] In the first column all the present forms (inf., pres. indic., pres. subj., etc.) are put in the inf. form. On the retention or loss of final *n* in the inf. and past partic. see § 8. The forms are all here given with the final *n*.

Of the verbs *abīden, arīsen, bīden, drīuen, grīpen* only present forms occur.

The form *rēpen* 'reaped', l. 43, corresponds to the *rǣpon* of the Chronicle (twelfth century Laud MS.) A.D. 1089, and possibly should be referred to an unrecorded verb **repan.*

CLASS II

Of the verbs *bēden, flēn, lōuten, rēwen, ssēten, tēn, vnlōuken* only present forms occur.

Inf.	Pret. Sg.	Pret. Pl.	Past Partic.
—	—	*flōten*	—
—	*lēs*	—	*ilōren*

CLASS III.

Inf.	Pret. Sg.	Pret. Pl.	Past Partic.
—	*bigan*	—	—
—	*braid*	—	—
drinken	*dranc*	—	—
finden	*fōnd, fūnde*	*fūnden*	*ifūnden*
—	*gan*	*gónne(n)*	—
singen	—	*sungen*	—
—	*sprōng*	—	—
—	*wan*	—	*iwónnen*
wórpen	—	*worpen*	—
wringen	*wrāng, wrōng*	—	—

Of the verbs *berewen, bīnden, helpen, swinken, wórpen* only present forms occur. *Forswolewe* has the weak past partic. *forswolewed.*

Class IV.

Inf.	Pret. Sg.	Pret. Pl.	Past Partic.
bẹ̄ren	*bar, bēr*	---	*bōren*
(to)brẹ̄ken	*brac*	—	—
(bi)cōmen	*(bi)cam*	*cōmen*	*icömen*
(bi)nimen	*nam*	*nōmen*	*inōmen*
(to)tẹ̄ren	*tar*	—	—

Class V.

Inf.	Pret. Sg.	Pret. Pl.	Past Partic.
bidden	*bad*	—	—
—	—	—	*bistẹ̄ken*
—	—	*frēten*	—
ȝiuen	*ȝaf*	---	*iȝiuen*
liġġen	*lai*	---	—
—	*quod*	—	—
(i)sēn	*(i)sauȝ*	*seyen, iseye*	—
sitten	—	*sēten*	—
spẹ̄ken	*spac*	—	—

Of the verbs *awrẹ̄ken, forȝiuen, mẹ̄ten* only present forms occur.

Class VI.

Inf.	Pret. Sg.	Pret. Pl.	Past Partic.
—	*awōc*	—	—
—	—	—	*ibāken*
drawen	—	*drôwen*	*òut-, todrawen*
fāren	—	—	---
—	*haf*	—	—

Class VI (*continued*).

Inf.	Pret. Sg.	Pret. Pl.	Past Partic.
lawȝen	—	—	—
—	—	—	*islawen*
—	*ssōk*	—	—
a-, vnderstǭnden	*stōd*	*stōden*	—
—	*swōr*	*swōre*	*iswǭren*
—	(*of*)*tōk*	—	—

The pret. *haf* is due to influence of verbs of Cl. V.

Reduplicating Verbs.

Inf.	Pret. Sg.	Pret. Pl.	Past Partic.
—	—	—	*anhǭngen*
bihǭlden	*at-, bihūld*	—	—
blǭwen	—	—	—
fallen	*fel*	*fellen*	*ifallen*
fōn, (*vnder*)*fǭngen*	*fēng*	—	*ifǭngen*
—	*bihēt*	—	*ihǭten*
knǭwen	*knēw*	—	—
lēten	*lēt, lette*	—	—
(*a*)*rēde*	—	—	—
—	—	—	*iswówen*
—	*vnfēld, vnfūld*	—	—

Is the form *fengeþ*, l. 135, miswritten for *fongeþ*?
Note the form *hatte* l. 80, *heiȝte* l. 384 = 'is called'.
The verbs *slēpen*, *wēpen*, have become weak.

§ 7. Anomalous verbs.

bēn. Inf. *bē*(*n*). Pres. ind. sing. 1. *am* (*bē* with future
meaning), 2. *art*, 3. *is* (*biþ, bēþ*[1] with future meaning),
plur. *bēþ.* Pres. subj. *bē.* Pret. sing. *was,* plur. *wēre.*
Pret. subj. *wēre.* P. P. *ibē.*

> With negation. Pres. ind. sing. 3. *nis.* Pret. sing. *nas,*
> plur. *nēre.*

dōn. Inf. *dō*(*n*). Imp. sing. *dō.* Pret. sing. and plur. *dude.*
P. P. *idō.*

gōn. Inf. *gō*(*n*). Pres. sing. 3. *gēþ, gōþ,* plur. *gōþ.* Imp.
sing. *gō.* P. P. *igō*(*n*).

wōle. Pres. sing. 1. *wōle, wōlle,* 2. *wōlt,* 3 *wōle,* plur. *wōlleþ.*
Pret. *wolde.* With negation. Pres. ind. sing. 1. *nellic* 3 ;
nellich 463 ; 2. *neltōu* 459. Pret. sing. and plur. *nolde*
219 ...

PRETERITE-PRESENT VERBS.

mai. Ind. pres. sing. 1. *mai,* 2. *miȝt,* 3. *mai,* plur. *mōwen.* Pres.
subj. *mōwe.* Pret. sing. *miȝte,* plur. *miȝten.*

mōt. Ind. pres. sing. 1. *mōt,* 2. *mōst,* 3. *mōt,* plur. *mōte*(*n*).

ssal. Ind. pres. sing. 1. *ssal,* 2. *ssalt,* 3. *ssal,* plur. *ssule*(*n*).
Pret. *ssolde.*

For the remaining preterite-present verbs see the Glossary
under *canst, darf, durste, ouȝte, wōt.*

§ 8. Endings of verbs.

Infinitive.

(i) At the end of the line the final *n* is regularly dropped,
the only exceptions being the monosyllabic forms *bēn, gōn,
isēn* (six instances) by the side of *bē, gō, isē, tē* (eight instances).

---

[1] This isolated sing. form should probably be read *biþ.*

(ii) In the caesura it is regularly dropped before a following consonant, but before a vowel or *h* it is sometimes retained (eight instances), sometimes dropped (eight instances).

(iii) In other positions it is regularly retained before vowels, the only exceptions being *cluppe* 7 216; *to sēch vs* 341. Before consonants it is regularly dropped (thirty-six instances); the *n* forms only occur eight times: *gǭn* 6; *cômen* 58; etc.

The *i* of the second class of weak verbs is found in the following cases: *hātie* 60, *lôuie*, 214, *gistni* 365, *gladien* 434, *þǭlie* 443. Cp. pres. indic. plur. *lôuieþ* 190.

Pres. Indic. 3rd Pers. Sg.

The regular ending is -*eþ* (-*þ*), fifty-seven instances. The syncopated *sit* occurs 31, 65, 67 ... ; *bihalt* 33; *ilast* 460.

Present Indic. Pl.

Ends regularly in -*eþ* (-*þ*), sixty-nine instances. The only exception is *côme* 118.[1] When followed by the personal pronoun the *þ* is, as usual, dropped: *wôlle ȝe* 1; etc.

Present Partic.

Ends in -*inde*: *wondrinde* 76; *blǭwinde* 230; *singinde* 521.

Pret. Indic. Pl.

Forms with final *n* largely predominate, the *n* being retained before consonants as well as before vowels. There are sixty-one instances of *n* forms, and only eleven without *n*.

Past Participle.

The strong past partic. regularly drops the *n* in the caesura and at the end of the lines, the only exception being the verb (*a*)*gǭn*, which has forms both with and without *n*: e.g. *igǭ* : *þǭ* 103, but *igǭn* : *anǭn*, 297. In other positions *n* forms

---

[1] Can the original have had *comeþ* : *frome* (an assonance), and did a copyist alter for the sake of the rhyme? We have a similar assonance in *bringe* : *vingres* 390.

are used before vowels and *h*, and forms without *n* before consonants. The only exception is *icômen bēþ* 476.

Both strong and weak participles have the prefix *i-*, except of course compound verbs : *idō* 62 ; *icôme* 66; *isēmed* 114 ; *itǭld* 133 ; etc.

§ 9. Substantives.

(i) *a*-stems. Masculine and neuter.

Dative Sg. The dative sg. has an inflexional *e*, which however can be dropped. At the end of the line *e* is regularly written when required for the rhyme, e. g. *flōde* (dat. sg.) : *gōde* (acc. pl.) 2 ; *telle* (inf.) : *spelle* (dat. sg.) 40; etc. It is regularly dropped when the rhyme word has no final *e* : *chin* : *in* 101 ; *mōd* (dat. sg.) : *gōd* (nom. sg.) 107 ; *ssróud* (dat. sg.) : *próud* (nom. sg.) 187; etc. In the caesura it is generally written : *drinke* 14; *lǭnde* 23, 25; etc. ; but in a number of cases it is dropped, and in most of these the line is best scanned as a septenary, in which the first half line normally ends in an accented syllable ; cp. *Nas néuere quéne ín þis lónd* 229 ; cp. also *lǭnd* 119; *dai* 265; etc. In other parts of the verse it is dropped before vowels and unemphatic *h* : e. g. *dich* 18; *lǭnd* 113; etc. But cp. *drinken* 317, where an *n* has been added. Before consonants it is not unfrequently dropped, and not always for metrical reasons, e. g. *wīn* 257 (*fúl of wín clér*). Disyllabic nouns do not take the final *e*, e. g. *hunger* 343; *water* 355; *lǭuerd* 435; *seluer* 507; etc. Compounds such as *wīnʒarde* 256 are treated as monosyllabic. The OE. neut. *swefn* appears not only in the dat. as *sweuene*, but also in the nom. acc. as *sweuene* 51 ..., *swefne* 35 ..., besides *sweuen* 120 ...

The neuter substantives either form their plural like the masc. in *-es*, as in *wōrdes* 1; etc.; or, as in OE., without inflexion, as in *ʒēr* 314, 499; *kȳn* 287 ... In *wēpnen* 350 we have a weak pl.

A dat. pl. in *e* occurs in *dawe* 13; *lifdawe* 24, 309.

(ii) *ō*-stems. Feminine.

The nom., dat., acc. sg. ends in *e*: *blisse* 354; etc. The plur. ends in *-es*: *strētes* 146; *pīnes* 337.

Verbal nouns in *ing* form the nom., dat., acc. sg. either with or without the *-e*: *tīdinge* (nom.) 537, (acc.) 206; *tīding* (nom.) 157, (acc.) 71; *blessinge* (acc.) 444; *mēting* (nom.) 90.

The dat. *world* occurs l. 19.

(iii) *i*-stems. Masculine.

The gen. pl. we have in *Egipte* 116, 119 ... beside *Egiptene* 143.

(iv) *u*-stems. Masculine and Feminine.

The masc. *u*-stems have gone over to the *a* declension, except that *sône* has the *-e* in the nom. acc. as well as in the dat. Pl. *sônes* 26 ...

The fem. *u*-stem *hǭnd* occurs in the dat. sg. *hǭnd* 141, acc. sg. *hǭnd* 133. The pl. is *hǭnden* 132, 335 ... In ll. 109, 185 the pl. *hǭnde* occurs in the rhyme.

(v) *r*-stems.

fader forms its dat. without *e*, e. g. 35 ... The gen. sg. *fader* occurs 67, 98, 504, 523, besides *faderes* 383. The gen. sg. *mōder* occurs 155. The pl. of *brōþer* is *brēþren* 42, 57, 59 ...

(vi) *n*-stems.

These have *e* in the nom., dat., acc. sg. The gen. does not occur. The pl. ends in *-(e)n*: *aldren* 13; *sterren* 50, 476; *fọ̄n* 74; *assen*, 114, 344 ... ; *mòwen* 357. The *n* has been dropped for the sake of the rhyme in *eye* 267 (or is it sg.?).

A gen. pl. in -*ene* occurs once : *prūdene* 508. *Lę̄uedis* 153 is
the only instance of an *s* plural.

(vii) Other consonant stems.

Niȝt is generally unaltered in the dat. sg: 320, 322 ..., but
niȝte occurs once, l. 254. Plurals : *children* 395; *men* 5. The
dat. pl. of *fōt* occurs as *fēt* 46, 58; the forms *fōte* 50, 455 and
fōt 48, 67 are presumably dat. sg.

§ 10. Adjectives.

(i) STRONG.

Adjectives which in OE. end in a consonant take no ending
in the nom. sg.: *heiȝ* 19 ; *dēþ* 95; *feir* 125; etc.

The dat. sg. ends in *e* : *ǭne* 2, 4, 80, 127 ...; *rēu(þ)fule*
30, 418 ; *nǭne* 38 ; *gōde* 85 ; *lǭnge* 127 ; *guldene* 412; etc.
Exceptions are *heiȝ* 125 ; *muchel* 250, 381 (besides *muchele*
232); *ōþer* 532.

The acc. sg. generally has *e* : *feire* 5 ; *grę̄te* 115 ; *ǭne gōde*
128; *guldene* 401 ; etc.   Acc. forms without *e* are less numer-
ous ; the instances are *gōd* 192 ; *richest* 207; *nǭn* 239, 334,
380; *such* 328; *al* 449, 511; *inōuȝ* 452. It is noteworthy that
most of these acc. forms without *e* are accompanied by nouns
which in OE. were neuter.

Adjectives which in OE. ended in -*ig* take no *e* either in the
dat. or acc.   Instances are : Dat. *sǭri* 107; *mani* 155; *þēstri*
243; etc.   Acc. *meri* 5; *sǭri* 239; *muri* 255; etc.

An archaic acc. is *nę̄nne* 235.

In the plural all cases end in *e* : *gōde* 1; *alle* 32; 45, 61; *heie*
146; *prōute* 146 ; etc.   The only exceptions are *lǭng* 146 (it
follows and is separated from its noun and moreover stands
in the rhyme); *ōþer* 286.

The only instance of an OE. adj. in -*ig* taking the *e* is *manie*
181. When used predicatively the adjectives appear in the pl.
both with and without *e* : *fulle* 17; *wīse* 123; *wōd* 15; *wīs* 129.
At the end of the line the *e* is added or dropped to suit the
rhyme.

(ii) Weak.

All cases of both numbers end in *e* : sg. *ẹ̄lde* 31, 169, 335;
ʒunge 34, 332; etc. ; pl. *fulle*, 74; *ʒunge* 392; etc. Adjectives
which in OE. ended in -*ig* drop the *e* : *sọ̄ri* 457. In the case
of *þis smal chaf* 330, we should probably read *smāle*.

§ 11. Pronouns.

(i) Personal Pronouns.

First person.

Sg. Nom. *ich* (written in the MS. *i°*) 21, 22 ... It is joined
    to the verb in *nellic* 3; *telli* 49; *nabbi* 309; *nellich*
    (not -*i°*) 463; *haddich* 477; *seidich* 485.

Dat. Acc. *mē*.

Pl. Nom. *wē*.

Dat. Acc. *vs*.

Second person.

Sg. Nom. *þou* 42 ... ; *þū* 82 ... After *t* : *tou* 38, 459.

Pl. Nom. *ʒē* 1, 124 ... Gen. *ʒoure* 'of you' 487. Dat.
    Acc. *ʒou* 3 ... ; *ou* 22.

Third person.

Sg. Masc. Nom. *hē*.

      Dat. *him*.

      Acc. *him* 36 ... ; *hine* 61, 137, 242, 465.

Sg. Fem. Nom. *hēo* 196, 216, 217 ...   Cp. also *nadda*
            334, 'she had not'.
     Dat. *hire* 196.
  Neut. Nom. Acc. *hit*.
Pl. Nom. *hī* 14, 17 ... (fifty-six instances); *þei* (five times)
            15, 46, 115, 262, 455.
    Dat. Acc. *hem* 6, 33, 44 ...   Cp. *brouȝtem* (=*brouȝte*
         hem) 368 ; *grettem* 91.

(ii) INDEFINITE PRONOUN.

me 'one' occurs 36, 270, 304, 327.

(iii) POSSESSIVE PRONOUNS.

First person singular.

Sg. Nom. *mī* 37, 42, 51 ...
    Dat. *mī* 48, 178, 302 ... ; *mīne* 40, 205.
Pl. *mī* 46, 309 ; *mīne* 42.

mī is used both in sg. and pl. when the possessive stands
in the thesis, and *mīne* when in the arsis.   See § 13.

First person plural.

* oure* 11, 13 ..., *vre* 72, 384.

Second person singular.

Sg. Nom. *þī* 52, 54 ... ; *þīn* 217, 319.
    Dat. Acc. *þī* 208, 298 ... ; *þine* 211, 299 ; *þin* 267, 319.
Pl. Nom. Dat. Acc. *þine* 57, 58, 70, 71.

Second person plural.

ȝoure 45 ...

Third person singular.

Masc. *his* 4 ...   Once in the pl. *hise* 86.
Fem. *hire* 176 ... With the *e* elided before a vowel, *hir* 195.

Third person plural.
here 14 ...

(iv) DEFINITE ARTICLE.

The regular form is *þe* 7 ..., which after *t* becomes *te* 48. Cp. also *atte* 94, 104, 111, 117, and *tę̄rnde* 87. It appears coalesced with the following word in *þǭnes* (= *þe ǭnes*) 402 and *tę̄rnde* 87. Traces of the old inflexions occur in *þane* (acc. sg.) 436; *þene* 301, 425; *þen* (acc.) 298, 302; *to þe nāle* (= *þen āle* dat.) 6; *to þe nēndinge* 29; *atte nēnde* 327.

þat has the force of the definite article (= *the*) in *þat chīld* 66, 67, 77, 79, 102, 135; *þat ǭ brōþer* 94, 103; *þat gamen* 108; *þat fē* 135.

(v) DEMONSTRATIVE PRONOUN.

þis. The regular form is *þis* for all cases of both sg. and plur. Instances of the plural are 63, 105, 121 ... After *t* it becomes *tis* 20. In the dat. sg. we also have *þisse* 197, 293, 294; *þissen* 341. By the side of the regular plural form *þis* the form *þēse* occurs five times 218, 337, 374, 409, 417.

§ 12. Age and dialect.

The MS. seems to have been written soon after the middle of the thirteenth century ; it cannot be earlier, as the spellings *o* for OE. *u* and *ou* for OE. *ū* show. Cp. Napier, *Holy Rood-Tree*, E.E.T.S. p. 85, and Morsbach, § 121.

The composition of the poem may be assigned to the same period.

The dialect is that of the South-west. The verbal endings prove its Southern origin; the pres. indic. pl. in -*eþ* (-*þ*); retention of the *i* in *hatie* 60, etc.; the ending of the pres. partic. in -*inde*.

The initial *v* for *f* in *vader* 39, etc., also shows that it was written in the South. That its home was the South-west and not South-east is proved by the treatment of OE. *ӯ*; cp. § 5 (7) and (12). Cp. also note to *sungen*, 486.

§ 13. Metre.

The metre of *Iacob and Iosep* consists of a mixture of Septenaries and Alexandrines, a metrical form characteristic of the thirteenth century and found in the *Passion of our Lord, The Woman of Samaria*, etc.[1] The Septenary has seven arses or stresses with a caesura after the fourth. The Alexandrine has six arses with the caesura after the third. In *Iacob and Iosep* the Alexandrines predominate considerably.

The first half of the Septenary ends in an arsis (cp. 5 *whíle men lóueden méri sóng, gámen and féire tále*).

The second half of the Septenary ends in a thesis, the preceding syllable being long (5 *gámen and féire tále*), more rarely in an arsis (20 *múchel ne óuerstéiȝ*).

The first half line of the Alexandrine ends in a thesis pre-

---

[1] I adopt Schipper's view.   Some scholars (Heuser, Kaluza) regard these poems as composed in Septenaries only, assuming that any unaccented syllable when followed by another unaccented syllable or standing in a pause (caesura or end of verse) can receive a secondary accent and form an arsis, e. g. 202 *Iósep cám to bóurè*; 204 '*Iósep*', *qúod þe quéne*.

ceded by a long syllable (1 *Wólle ʒe nóu ihére*).   The few
exceptions where it apparently ends in an arsis, such as 26
sónes hé wan tén, can, as Heuser pointed out, be made
correct by a slight emendation : *sónes hé wan tén*[*e*]. The
second half of the Alexandrine can end in a thesis, as
in 1 *wórdes swíþe góde,* or in an arsis as in 31 *Iácob þe
élde mán.*

In the case of both metres the thesis can be disyllabic, as
in 5 *whíle men lóueden méri sóng,* or can be wanting, e.g. 15
þei wéren ríʒt wód ; 40 *of míne mélínge* ; 46 7 *tó mi fét fálle.*

In at least three instances the line seems overloaded :

81 *Ac lutel er hi weren in Sichem bi hem ich stod þo.*

314 *Ac þou ssalt habbe raþer seue ʒer blisse of alle gode.*

512. *7 seggeþ þat Iosep is in Egipte ase heiʒ as a king.*

And it is possible that some emendation is required.   Heuser
would omit *lutel* 81, *raþer* 314, *7 seggeþ* 512 (emending *þing*
to *tiþing* in the previous line).   But such changes are not
certain.

Rhyme.

(1) Normal close *ē* (WS. *ǣ,* Angl. *ē,* from WG. *ā*) rhymes
with close *ē* from OE. *ē* : *wēre* : *hēre* (OE. *hēr*) 41 ; *wēpeþ*
(OE. *wēpeþ*) : *forlēteþ* 137 ; *swēte* (OE. *swēte*) : *lēte* 535.   But
it also rhymes with open *ę̄,* from OE. *ǣ* (WG. *ai*) and OE. *ēa* :
lę̄de (WG. *ai*) : *arēde* 119 ; *lę̄de* (WG. *ai*) : *rēde* 183 ; *slēpe* :
mę̄te (WG. *ai*) 254 ; *biwēued* : *hę̄ued* (OE. *ēa*) 425 ; *lę̄deþ*
(WG. *ai*) : *grēdeþ* 465 ; *biwēued* : *birę̄ued* (OE. *ēa*) 517.

(2) Close *ō* rhymes with open *ǭ* : *wǭt* : *fōt* 47 ; *rǭpe* : *wōpe*
127 ; *blōdi* : *sǭri* 171.

(3) Short vowels sometimes rhyme with long ones : *wīs*

ĭs 129; *ĭs* : *grīs* 113, 208; *þerŏn* : *agǭn* 318; *ǭn* : *mă̆n*[1] 131; etc.

(4) Assonances are not infrequent: *wǭmbe* : *lǭnge* 7 ; *sône* : *côme* 53, 65, 155, 159; *ēk* : *fēt* 57 ; *hine* : *binime* 61 ; *sprǭng* : *lǭnd* 157 ; *blōdi* : *sǭri* 171 ; *līue* : *blīþe* 177, 212, 348 ... ; *wēpeþ* : *fôrlēteþ* 137; *slēpe* : *mę̄te* 254; *hǭm* : *mǭn* 330, 431 ; *hǭm* : *igǭn* 346 ; *icôme* : *lôue* 378 ; *aჳein*[2] : *drę̄m* 417 ; *anǭn* : *hǭm* 429.   Cp. also *bringe* : *fingres* 390.

(5) Assonances also occur where the vowels differ in length: *lif* : *wiþ* 195; *hǭm* : *mă̆n*[1] 31.

(6) The rhyme *wēpe* : *wīpe* 489 is inexact.

[1] Read *mŏn*.   [2] Read *aჳēn*?

[IACOB AND IOSEP]¹

Wolle ȝe nou ihere wordes swiþe gode
Of one patriarke after Noees flode?
Nellic ȝou nouȝt tellen of þis flodes grame,
Bote of one patriarke, Iacob was his name.
While men loueden meri song, gamen 7 feire tale;   5
Nou hem is wel leuere gon to þe nale,
Vcchen out þe gurdel 7 rume þe wombe,
Comen erliche þider 7 sitte þer ful longe.
Þat is þe soule ful loþ, 7 lef þe licame,
Bote we hit bileuen, hit biþ a luþer game.   10
To fullen oure wombe hit is lutel pris,
7 seþþe ligge slepe, such hit were a gris.
Þus ferden oure aldren bi Noees dawe,
Of mete 7 of drinke hi fulden here mawe;
7 for ȝiuernesse þei weren riȝt wod;   15
For þi sende oure Louerd Noees flod.
Þo hi miȝten drinke þat hi weren fulle,
Hi floten swiþe riued bi dich 7 bi pulle.
Þer nas in þis world hul non so heiȝ,
Þat tis vnirude flod muchel ne ouersteiȝ.   20
Nou ich wole fon on þer ich er let,
7 tellen ou of Iacob, so ich ȝou bihet.
Iacob liuede in londe 7 louede Godes lawe
So dude Ysaac his fader bi his lifdawe.
Iacob liuede in londe, 7 feire he ladde his lif,   25
Sones he wan ten on Lya his wif;

¹ No heading in MS.

On Rachel he wan tweye, Iosep 7 Beniamin.
Betere is for to here þis tale þen to drinke win ;   [f. 1^b]
For whoso hereþ þis tale to þe nendinge,
Of more reufule song herde he neuere singe.   30
Nou he sit in halle, Iacob þe elde man,
7 his sones alle from felde comeþ hom.
Iacob bihalt his sones, of hem he was bliþe ;
7 Iosep þe ȝunge bigan to speke swiþe.
His fader he tolde a swefne aniȝt þat him mette   35
7 bad swiþe ȝerne telle þat me him lette.
'Do nou, mi sone dere, God leue þe so to speke,
þat tou in none worde his heste ne tobreke.'
'Vader,' seide Iosep, 'nou ich wole þe telle
Of mine metinge 7 of mine spelle.   40
Me þuȝte, ase ich slepte, afeld þat we were,
þou 7 mi moder 7 mine breþren here ;
7 so we repen oure corn 7 oure sseues knetten,
7 vpriȝt in þe felde wel feire we hem setten,
Me þuȝte þat ȝoure sseues, þer hi stoden alle,   45
To me þei gonnen louten 7 to mi fet falle.
Ȝit me þuȝte an oþer, fader, God hit wot,
þat te sunne 7 þe mone fellen to mi fot.
Ȝit me þuȝte þe þridde, fader, telli þe,
þat elleue sterren to fote fellen me.   50
þis is mi sweuene, fader, þát ich telle þe,
Ȝif hit þi wille were, ared what hit mai be.'
þenne seide Iacob to Iosep his sone,
'Tide wat bitide, ȝit wole þi swefne come.
Tide wat bitide, ȝit wole þi swefne be.   [f. 2]   55
Ich wene mid iwisse, ȝut we hit ssulen ise,
þat ich 7 þi moder 7 þine breþren ek
Moten for fine nede comen to þine fet.'

Þis iherden his breþren, þerfore hem was ful wo,
Hi gonnen hatie Iosep ase here fulle fo.   60
Þau alle[1] his ten breþren þerfore hateden hine,
Þat oure Louerd wole habben ido mai no man binime.
Þis breþren wendeþ afeld to witen here fe,
Ac Iosep leuede at hom, þat hende was 7 fre.
Iacob sit in halle 7 clepeþ Iosep his sone;   65
Þat child swiþe sone to his fader is icome.
At his fader fot þat child him sit akne,
7 axeþ him wel feire wat his wille be.
Sone seide Iacob, 'Wende þou most afeld
To seche þine breþren, 7 wer be here teld.   70
Bring vs hom tiding hu þine breþren fare.
Vre Louerd, þat is in heuene, berewe þe from care.'
Iosep geþ afeldward, euel ne þouȝte he non,
He wende to sechen his breþren, 7 souȝte his fulle fon.
He secheþ hem, ne mai he hem finde, þerfore him was wo;
Þenne fond a man al one þe child wondrinde go.   76
Þis man axede þat child woder he wolde te;
Iosep his breþren secheþ 7 fain hem wolde ise.
Þe man onswerede þat child, 7 þus he spac to him,
'Hi beþ in one felde, hatte Dotaym;   80
Ac lutel er hi weren in Sichem, bi hem ich stod þo.
Child, ȝif þou hem wolt finde, to Dotaym þu go.   [f. 2ᵇ
Child, ȝif þou hem wolt finde, to Dotaym þu go riȝt,
Also ich vnderstonde, þer þu hem finde miȝt.'
Iosep mid gode wille þiderward he geþ,   85
Þer alle hise ten breþren habbeþ isworen his deþ.
He cam toward his breþren, þat ternde ssolde bere,
Hi siggeþ hem bitwene, 'Her comeþ þe metere.

---

[1] alle] MS. allae.

Nime we 7 quellen þis ilke hinderling,
7 lokeþ wat hi*m* ssal helpe þerafter his meting. '   90
He cam to his breþren 7 grettem eu*er*uchon ;
Hi þencheþ al an oþer, 7 gripeþ hi*m* anon.
Quellen hi*m* hi wolleþ, nou hi hi*m* habbeþ inome,
Ac Ruben, þat o broþer, he spac atte frome,
' A deþ pet is her bisides þat water er þis i*n* stod ;   95
Worpeþ þeri*n*ne Iosep, ssende we nouʒt oure blod,'
(Iosep for to helpe Ruben spac þis tale)
' Ʒif we þis child aquelleþ, hit beþ oure fader bale.'
His fader hi*m* ʒaf a kurtel þat rum was 7 wid,
Wel hit bicam þe child, hit was hi*m* fotsid.   100
Hi strupten of þe curtel, of swere 7 of chin,
Al naked i*n* þe pette hi worpen þat child in.
Ac Ruben, þat o broþer, þe*n*ne he is igo,
Ne miʒte he for reuþe atte pette be þo.
Þis oþre sitteþ bisides 7 foþ on here mete,   105
Þencheþ hi neiþer of serewe ne of hete.
Iosep sit i*n* pette mid ful sori mod,
His breþren lawʒeþ loude, þat gamen hem þinkeþ god.
Nou Iosep sit in pette 7 wri*n*geþ his honde.   [f. 3]
A wey, þat bitwene breþren ssal be þus muchel onde !   110
Nou drawen him vp hi wolleþ, 7 quellen hi*m* atte frome,
Þe*n*ne seien hi bisides twei riche chapmen come.
Vrom a lond hi comen, Galaad ihoten is,
Mid here assen isemed of fer 7 of gris.
Of stor 7 of spices þei ladden grete male   115
Into Egipte lond to sullen hit to sale.
Þe*n*ne spac hi*m* Iuda, he spac atte frome,
' Wolle we sullen Iosep þis chapmen þat here come ?
Fer i*n*to Egypte lond hi hi*m* wolleþ lede,
Þe*n*ne worþ his sweuen eþ to arede,'   120

Hi comen to þis chapmen 7 sseweden here tale,
Iosep in þe pette hi chepeden to sale.
Þis chapmen beþ wise 7 axeþ wer he be.
'Comeþ ner,' hi seiden, '7 ȝe him mowen ise ;
Hit is a swiþe feir child 7 of kunne heiȝ.'   125
Mid þat ilke worde þe pet hi weren neiȝ.
Hi drowen vp Iosep mid one longe rope,
Ac one gode while ne miȝte he speke for wope.
Þis chapmen biholdeþ Iosep, þat beþ swiþe wis,
7 Iosep to begge swiþe lef hem is.   130
Hi chepeþ 7 hi bedeþ, sone hi beþ at on.
Iosep wrang his honden 7 was ful sori man.
Hi casten hond to purse, þe panes beþ itold ;
Nou helpe Crist Iosep, so ȝung he is isold.
Þis chapmen fengeþ þat child, þis breþren þat fe ;   135
Darf no man axe wer Iosep sori be ;   [f. 3ᵇ]
For euere ase hi hine ledeþ, euer he wepeþ,
His fader 7 his moder ȝung he forleteþ.
Þis chapmen beþ wel bliþe þat Iosep habbeþ ibouȝt,
7 vpon þe sestronde hi him habbeþ ibrouȝt.   140
Þis chapmen nimeþ Iosep riȝt bi þe hond,
7 so hi ledeþ Iosep into Egipte lond.
Ac of Egiptene speche couþe he no þing,
For þi he wepte sore, þis ilke ȝungling.
Hi ladden Iosep into þe burȝ, þat riche was 7 strong : 145
Castles heie 7 proute, stretes wide 7 long,
Mani feir halle 7 mani feir bour,
Whit so eni lilie, briȝt so eni flour.
Muche was þe blisse þat was in þe burȝ,
Iosep for to sullen hi ladden þurȝ 7 þurȝ.   150
Þider comen kniȝtes 7 burgeis ful bolde,
Hi comen into þe strete Iosep to biholde.

Leuedis of boure 7 maidenes fre
Comen into þe strete Iosep to ise.
Ac þer þuȝte muche wonder mani a moder sone,   155
Hem þuȝte hit was an angel from heuene icome.
Ful sone þe tiding of Iosep hit sprong
To Putifar þe stiward of Egipte lond.
Putifar þe stiward þider he is icome,
7 in his ferade mani a kniȝtes sone.   160
So sone so þe stiward on Iosep bihuld,
He liȝte of his stede, his mantel he vnfuld,
Cofre he lette vnlouke 7 gold casten out anon,   [f. 4]
Sone he bouȝte Iosep of þis chapmon.
More þen he axede for Iosep he ȝaf,   165
7 seþþen on his stede wel feire he him haf.
Nou lete we Iosep ride, God ssilde him from care,
7 vte we speken of Iacob his fader, hou he fare.
Nou he sit in halle, Iacob þe elde man,
7 his sones ten from¹ felde comeþ hom,   170
7 Ioseppes curtel hi bringeþ al blodi,
Þo Iacob hit gan biholde iwis he was sori.
Þo he sauȝ his kurtel ispreind al wiþ blod,
Nas neuere for his child fader so sorimod.
Adoun he fel iswowe 7 tar his hore loc,   175
Þe moder feng to renden hire neb 7 hire smoc.
Euer seide þe moder, 'Wo is me a liue,
For mi sone Iosep be ich neuere bliþe.'
Euere seide Iacob, 'Iosep is islawe,
Oþer summe luþere deres habbeþ him todrawe.'   180
Þider comen manie of fremede 7 o kinne
For to gladen Iacob, ac his sones hadden sinne.
Woso seye Iacob his sorinesse lede,

                    ¹ MS. fron.

Hit were muche reuþe in boc for to rede.
Nou Iacob sit in halle 7 wringeþ his honde,   185
We ssule speken of Iosep in Egipte londe.
Nou Putifar ssrudeþ Iosep mid dereworþe ssroud,
7 ȝiueþ him Pharaon þe king, mid him he is proud.
Nou is Iosep feir child in Pharaones halle,
Þe pore 7 þe riche louieþ him alle.   [f. 4ᵇ]   190
Tofore þe king selue he serueþ atte bord,
Of pore 7 of riche he haþ wel god word.
Hit fel in one daye, þe king was out iwent
To þe wode to ssete mid his bowe ibent.
Þe quene louede Iosep ase hir owe lif,   195
Heo sente him after sone to speken hire wiþ.
Ac of þisse þinge nuste Iosep riȝt nouȝt :
Aruȝ hit were to knowe alle wimmanes þouȝt.
Ac þer wimman is god, nis non so swete þing,
For al þat euere Eue brac in paradis   200
Oure leuedi hit bette, þat dereworþest is.
Iosep cam to boure, þat hende was 7 fre.
'Leuedi,' quod Iosep, 'wat þi wille be ?'
'Iosep,' quod þe quene, 'nou þou art welcome,
Nou in mine boure ich þe haue inome.   205
Ich þe wole tellen one tidinge,
Ich wole þe make richest man after oure kinge.
Þou ssalt habbe þi wil of fer 7 of gris,
Of gold 7 of seluer, of al þat feir is.
Þou ssalt haue þi wil of al Egipte londe,   210
Ssal neuere no man þine heste astonde.
7 of one þinge iwis þu miȝt be bliþe,
Þer nis no man me so lef þat euere is aliue.
Ȝif þou canst in boure louie me derne,
Þe prute of Egipte ssal þe nouȝt be werne.'   215

Mid þat ilke worde heo gan him cluppe 7 kisse.
'Iosep, ich am þin,' heo seide, 'mid iwisse.'   [f. 5]
Iosep of þese wordes nas he no þing glad,
He nolde in none wise don ase þe quene him bad.
Þeiȝ Iosep were in boure stille bisteke,   220
He nolde in none wise his trouþe tobreke.
Mid his white fingres hire armes he vnfeld,
7 wende from þe quene, ac his mantel heo athuld.
Heo braid of hire wimpel 7 loude feng to reme,
Þer come serians wel fele for to nime ȝeme,   225
Wat here leuedi miȝte be, þat hem was so lef.
'A! Lokeþ nou,' heo seide, 'þis Ebrewisse þef,
Of me he wende stille to habben his gome,
Nas neuere quene in þis lond ido so muche ssome.'
Þe king cam from þe wode mid blowinde beme,   230
Þe quene fel to his fet 7 loude feng to reme,
7 tolde þe king of þis muchele ssome,
Þunche hit no wonder þeiȝ he ne hadde grome.
Þe king him lette nime 7 ful faste binde :
Nou ne mai Iosep nenne frend finde.   235
Alle þat þis iherde þerfore weren ful wo :
Summe for þe quene, ac for Iosep wel mo.
Nou is Iosep so wo þat he not wat he mai :
Bide neuere no god man non so sori dai.
Ac heuede Iosep ido ase þe quene him bad,   240
He miȝte ben in halle mid oþre bliþe 7 glad.
Gulteles in þe pette his breþren hine dude,
7 gulteles he is nouþe in ful þestri stede.
Ac þer he is ful longe muche wo to abide,   [f. 5ᵇ]
Oure Louerd he hit þonkeþ, tide wat bitide.   245
Hit fel in one daye to þe newe ȝer,
Iwreyed was wel stronge þe kinges botiler,

Ase hi ferden here wai in þe morewentide
þene seȝen hi twolf ȝungemen after hem ride
and helm ⁊ mid brunie mid swerdes out diȝe
þo wenden þese ten breþren alle to ten islawe
Abideþ hi seiden þenes abideþ ȝe beþ inome
to fore þe stiward aȝein ȝe sulen alle come
for a guldene nap þ᷒ȝe habbeþ inome
ne ȝe in his londe mid þefþe beþ ifonge
ȝoure dom is idemed alle ȝe worþeþ anhonge
For ȝoure assen isemed al of rede golde
Of faraones lond þe king faren ȝe ne scolde
Alle þese ten breþren turneþ hem aȝein
and renkfule wepe ⁊ mid dreri drem
To fore þe stiward aȝein hi beþ alle ibrouȝt
þe nap in here sakke sone hit is isouȝt
þe nap is ifunde sone ⁊ anon
non wriȝeþ hi here honden his breþren euuch on
Iosep sauȝ his breþren wepe sore hit hi gan rewe
he nolde i none wise ȝit þat hi him knewe
Iosep feng þene nap mid pal he was biȝeued
he lokede on his breþren ⁊ scok on hem his heued
Awaried worþe swikedom ⁊ þat hit erst funde
So mani gultelese man hit bngeþ to þe grunde
þene seide iosep to his breþren anon
habbe ȝe he seide mo breþren athom
ȝe lord seide ruben a child þer is athom
for to gladen oure fader þ᷒makeþ muche mon

for a sone þᵗ he tes ⁊ louede so his lif
ne miȝte him selþe gladien his child no his wif
hi swore bi þilke loid þᵗ is heiȝ in heuene
more he louede þane sone þan vs alle elleuene
þ̄ene seide iosep wolle ȝe me ihere
ȝif ȝe of egipte lond wollet faren skere
Ich ȝou wolle tellen one tidiȝe
ȝe ssule make me siker þᵗ ilke child me briȝe
loid seide ruben we ssule ful fain
beniamin þe brigen ⁊ alle comen aȝein
⁊ þi dom þohe when we beþ icome
habbe we þe blessinge of oure fader inome
Iosep dranc to ruben mid ful riche wyn
⁊ alle hi pliȝten trouþe to brige beniamin.
feire fareþ þis ȝugemen bi daiȝ ⁊ biniȝt
to here fader iacob þᵗ hi comen riȝt
⁊ habbeþ to iacob al his corn ibrouȝt
þou haþ beniamin inoiȝ þᵗ erere he haþ bisouȝt
Iacob of his corn was swiþe glad
þou haþ beniamin inoiȝ þᵗ he er bad
Iacob of his corn aboute sende anon
to frendes þᵗ for huger maden muche mon
Ac alle hise ten breþren to sote þei beþ ifalle
þe trouþe þᵗ hi pliȝten hi hi telleþ alle
þo iacob iherde þis sori odinge
Adoun he fel iswoȝe his honden he gan to rige
A wher artou mi deþ whi neltou me fonge:

7 þe kinges baxtere iwreyed was ful stronge.
To Iosep hi beþ icast, 7 þer hi liggeþ longe,
7 in þe prison liggeþ mid ful muchel wronge.   250
Nabbeþ hi none blisse of harpe ne of songe,
Of olde ne of ȝunge, of fremede ne of sibbe,
Leuere hem were to be ded þen so longe to libbe.
Hit fel in one niȝte þe botiler feng to slepe,
A swiþe muri sweuene him þuȝte þat he gan mete,   255
Þat in þe winȝarde þe kinges coupe he ber,
7 wrong hit of þe grapes ful of win cler.
Þe baxtere mette an oþer, nas hit nouȝt so god,
In þe bachuse him þuȝte þat he stod,
Of bred he fulde a basket 7 to þe halle he wolde hit bere,
Þe foules bi þe lifte hit gonnen al totere.   261
Amorewen ase þei seten wiþ Iosep atte bord,
Here sweuen hi him tolden word after word.
Iosep here sweuen sone haueþ arouȝt.
'Ȝe ssulen in þis þridde dai of prison ben ibrouȝt.   265
Þou ssalt, sir baxtere, anhonged be ful heye,
Foules bi þe lifte holen out þin eye.
Þou ssalt, sire botiler, þi mester vnderfonge,
Wiþ alle worssipe mest þe king serue longe.
7 wen me serueþ þe king mid harpe 7 mid songe,   270
Þench on seli Iosep, þat her liþ mid wrronge.'   [f. 6]
Also ase Iosep seide, also hit bicam :
Þe botiler of Iosep lute ȝeme nam,
Þat in þe prison liþ mid ful muche wronge.
Naþ he none blisse of harpe ne of songe,   275
Of olde ne of ȝunge, of fremede ne of sibbe,
Leuere him [1] were to be ded þen so longe to libbe.

---

[1] MS. *hem.*

Wel ouȝte we to heren¹ him þat is riȝtwis,
7 nou ȝe mowen ihere hou hende oure Louerd is,
Hou feire he sende help to Iosep þe ȝungling   280
Þurȝ a sweuene þat mette Pharaon þe king.
Þe king ase he slepte him þuȝte þat he rod
In a medewe grene þat long was 7 brod.
Seue kuin fatte him þuȝte þat he sauȝ gon:
So fatte ne so feire sauȝ he neuere non.   285
Oþer seue lene toȝeines hem gonne gon
·7 frete þe seue fatte kyn eueruchon.
Þo þe seue fatte kin alle forswolewed were,
Þe seue kin lene neuere þe fullore nere.
Amorewen þe king awoc, his sweuen he tolde   290
Vrles 7 barons 7 burgeis ful bolde.
Ac þer nas neiþer baron ne kniȝt
Þat of þisse þinge couþe reden him aiwiȝt.
Þo herde þe botiler of þisse sweuene speke,
Þo þouȝte he furst on Iosep, þat so longe lai bisteke. 295
He cam to þe kinge 7 tolde him anon
Of him 7 of þe baxtere hou hit was igon.
'Louerd, of þi sweuene ȝif he ne seiþ þen ende²,   [f. 6ᵇ]
Do me, Louerd, aȝein into þine bende.'
Þenne seide Faraon, Faraon þe king,   300
'Let bringe bifore me þene ȝungling.
Ȝif he of mi sweuene seiþ me þen ende,
Al his gult ich him forȝiue 7 quite faten³ of bende.'
Forþ me feccheþ Iosep, þat bloc was 7 lene,
Durste for þe quene no man him bimene.   305
'Louerd,' seide Iosep, 'ich hit þonke þe,
Nou ich wot mid iwisse islawe þat ich ssal be,

---

¹ MS. *wheren*.   ² MS. *þenende*.   ³ *faten* altered from
faren.

Nou ic*h* wot mid iwisse þat ic*h* ssal ben islawe,
For nabbi none blisse of mi lifdawe.'
Ac þe ki*n*g wel feire his sweuen he tolde,   310
7 bad swiþe feire reden þat he hit ssolde.
'Lou*er*d,' seide Iosep, 'þi sweuen is eþ to telle,
Oure Lou*er*d wole in þi lond muche p*r*ude felle[1].
Ac þou ssalt habbe raþer seue 3er blisse of alle gode
Þur3 a swete water ssal comen of Niles flode.   315
Þou ssalt haue þenne[2] hu*n*ger 7 hete,
Wone of alle gode, of d*r*inken[3] 7 of mete.
Þis is þi sweuene, sire ki*n*g, þench þou þeron,
Bote C*r*ist be þin help, Egipte is al agon.'
Heron þe king þencheþ bi ni3t 7 bi dai,   320
Not he a liue what he do mai.
Heron þe king þencheþ bi dai 7 bi ni3t,
Me ne couþe of þis þinge reden hi*m* no wi3t.
Þe*n*ne spac an old man þat was wis of speche.[4]

.   .   .   .   .

We*n*ne ic*h* þenche on Abraham, hou he gan þider wende: [f. 7]
Muche þo þolede Abraham ssame mid his wiue,   326
7 seþþen atte nende of lond me gan him d*r*iue.
7 we*n*ne þe ri3twise man þolede such ssome,
Into Egipte to sende þu*n*cheþ me no gome.
Ofte of þis smal chaf þis breþren brou3ten hom,   330
7 for wone of mete maden muche mon.
Beniamin þe 3u*n*ge bad his moder bred,
7 seide he was afingred þat he was nei3 ded.
Þe moder swor swiþe þat bred nadda non,
Þo wrong he his honden, Iacob þe elde man,   335
For leu*er*e were Iacob of liue for to ben

---

[1] MS. *falle.*   [2] *þenne*] MS. *þer.*   [3] The *k* altered from
another letter.   [4] Between foll. 6 and 7 a leaf has been cut out.

Þen bi Beniamin þe ȝunge þese pines isen.
Ȝit Beniamin þe ȝunge makeþ muche mon
Þenne clepede Iacob his sones eueruchon.
'Sones,' seide Iacob, 'Nede ȝe mote wende   340
For to sech vs corn in þissen estende.
For betere ȝou is to swinke 7 erne ȝoure mete
Þenne at hom to deye on hunger 7 on hete.
Nimeþ ȝoure assen 7 nimeþ ȝoure horn,
Nimeþ ȝou seluer 7 gold to buggen vs corn.   345
Ac Beniamin þe ȝunge bileue ssal at hom ;
Me reweþ euere Iosep þat afelde was igon.
For ȝif he hadde at hom bileued, ȝit he were aliue ;
For þe loue of Iosep be ich neuere bliþe.
Nimeþ ȝoure wepnen 7 wendeþ ȝoure wai,   350
Berewe ȝou from care oure Louerd, þat wel mai.'
Feire fareþ þis ȝunge men bi dai 7 bi niȝt   [f. 7ᵇ]
Into Egipte lond þat hi comen riȝt.
Muche was þe blisse 7 muche was þe gome
In water 7 in londe of wilde 7 of tome.   355
Muche was þe blisse þat hi þar iseye,
Bernes ful riche 7 mowen ful heye.
Muche was þe blisse after here swinke
Þat hi þare funden of mete 7 of drinke.
Hem oftok a menestral, his harpe he bar arugge.   360
'Whennes be ȝe, ȝunge men ? Ich bidde þat ȝe me sigge.
Me þuncheþ bi ȝoure assen þat corn ȝe wolde begge,
7 ich ȝou wole bringe to þe tubrugge.
Þar þe¹ hendeste man þat euere is aliue
Ȝou wole gistni toniȝt 7 make ȝou ful bliþe.   365
Ȝe þuncheþ ferrene men 7 alle freboren,
Toniȝt ssal mani kniȝtchild knele ȝou biforen.'

¹ þar þe] MS. parle.

He brouȝtem to þe castel ase he hem bihet,
7 spac wiþ þe porter in þat he hem let.
Hi seyen in þe castel mani riche þing,   370
7 Iosep sitten in halle, such hit were a king.
Ac if hi wenden Iosep þer for to sen,
Leuere hem were alle at hom on hunger ded to ben.
Alle þese ten breþren comen into þe halle,
Tofore Ioseppes fet akne hi valleþ alle.   375
'Ariseþ vp', seide Iosep, 'Sitte ȝe nouȝt akne,
Ac telleþ me wel feire wat ȝoure wille be.'
'From Ierusalem', quod Ruben, 'we beþ hider icome.
Let sullen vs corn, louerd, for Godes loue   [f. 8]
Old man is oure fader 7 corn naþ he non,   380
For muchel one nede we beþ hider igon.'
Þenne seide Iosep, such hit were his gome,
'Wat is', he seide, 'ȝoure faderes nome?'
'Vre fader heiȝte Iacob, vre moder Rachel.'
Mid þat ilke worde he knew hem ful wel.   385
Þo Iosep iherde þat his fader was aliue,
Nas neuere for his fader child also bliþe.
He goþ into þe boure 7 wepeþ for blisse,
Sore he is alonged his breþren to kisse.
Iosep cam into halle, þe water he lette bringe,   390
7 halde to here honden mid his wite vingres.
Feire beþ þis ȝunge men iserued þilke niȝt
Of mete ne of drinke trukede hem no wiȝt.
Iosep ful riche win lette to him bringe,
7 so he bad þis children on Ebrewisse singe.   395
7 so hi sungen alle ase Iosep hem bad,
Seþþe he cam into Egipte nas Iosep so glad.
Al of rede wete here assen he lette seme,
For to meten here corn nam he none ȝeme.

Nou dude Iosep a swiþe wonderþing,   400
He nam a guldene nap, was Pharaones þe king,
7 putte in þones sakke wiþinne þe prene,
7 þerof cam [1] þis ȝunge men swiþe muche tene.
Feire hi nomen leue to wenden here way
Toward here contre a lutel ere day.   405
Ase hi ferden here wai in þe morewentide,   [f. 8b]
Þenne seyen hi twolf ȝunge men after hem ride
Mid helm 7 mid brunie, mid swerdes outdrawe,
Þo wenden þese ten breþren alle to ben islawe.
'Abideþ', hi seiden, 'þeues, abideþ, ȝe beþ inome,   410
Tofore þe stiward aȝein ȝe ssulen alle come
For a guldene nap þat ȝe habbeþ inome.
Ȝif ȝe in þis londe mid þefþe beþ ifonge,
Ȝoure dom is idemed, alle ȝe worþeþ anhonge;
For ȝoure assen isemed al of rede golde   415
Of Faraones lond þe king faren ȝe ne ssolde.'
Alle þese ten breþren turneþ hem aȝein
Mid reuþfule wepe 7 mid dreri drem,
Tofore þe stiward aȝein hi beþ alle ibrouȝt,
Þe nap in here sakke sone hit is isouȝt.   420
Þe nap is ifunde sone 7 anon,
Nou wringeþ hi here honden þis breþren eueruchon.
Iosep sauȝ his breþren wepe, sore hit him gan rewe,
He nolde in none wise ȝit þat hi him knewe.
Iosep feng þene nap, mid pal he was biweued,   425
He lokede on his breþren, 7 ssok on hem his heued.
Awaried worþe swikedom 7 þat hit erest funde,
So mani gultelese man hit bringeþ to þe grunde.
Þenne seide Iosep to his breþren anon,

---

[1] cam] MS. come

'Habbe ȝe', he seide, 'mo breþren at hom?'   430
'Ȝe, louerd', seide Ruben, 'a child þer is at hom
For to gladen oure fader, þat makeþ muche mon
For a sone þat he les 7 louede so his lif,   [f. 9]
Ne miȝte him seþþe gladien his child no his wif.'
Hi swore bi þilke louerd þat is heiȝ in heuene,   435
'More he louede þane sone þan vs alle elleuene.
Þenne seide Iosep, 'Wolle ȝe me ihere,
Ȝif ȝe of Egiþte lond wolleþ faren skere,
Ich ȝou wolle tellen one tidinge,
Ȝe ssule make me siker þat ilke child me bringe.'   440
'Louerd,' seide Ruben, 'we ssule ful fain
Beniamin þe bringen 7 alle comen aȝein
7 þi dom þolie when we beþ icome,
Habbe we þe blessinge of oure fader inome.'
Iosep dranc to Ruben mid ful riche win,   445
7 alle hi pliȝten trouþe to bringe Beniamin.
Feire fareþ þis ȝunge men bi dai 7 bi niȝt
To here fader Iacob þat hi comen riȝt.
7 habbeþ to Iacob al þis corn ibrouȝt:
Nou haþ Beniamin inouȝ þat eror he haþ bisouȝt.   450
Iacob of þis corn was swiþe glad:
Nou haþ Beniamin inouȝ þat he er bad.
Iacob of þis corn aboute sende anon
To frendes þat for hunger maden muche mon.
Ac alle þis¹ ten breþren to fote þei beþ ifalle,   455
Þe trouþe þat hi pliȝten hi him telleþ alle.
Þo Iacob iherde þis sori tidinge,
Adoun he fel iswowe, his honden he gan wringe.
'A! wher artou, mi deþ, whi neltou me fonge?
Nou mi wrecchede lif ilast al to longe.   [f. 9ᵇ] 460

¹ þis] MS. *hise*. Cp. note.

Iloren ich haue Iosep, þat ich louede so swiþe,
7 nou ich ssal Beniamin, be ich neuere bliþe.
Ac nellich nouȝt, mine sones, ȝoure trouþe þat ȝe breke,
Oure Louerd, wen his wille is, wel he me mai awreke.'
Þis breþren nimeþ Beniamin 7 forþ hi hine ledeþ,   465
Iacob falleþ iswowe 7 for serewe gredeþ.
Feire fareþ þis ȝunge men bi dai 7 bi niȝt
Into Egipte lond þat hi comen riȝt.
Hi comen into þe castel þer Iosep was in,
Ruben him bitecheþ his broþer Beniamin.   470
Þo Iosep isauȝ his breþren alle elleuene,
Him þuȝte þat he was bliþore þen þauȝ he were in heuene.
He goþ into þe boure 7 wepeþ for blisse,
Sore he is alonged his breþren to kisse.
'Louerd,' seide Iosep, 'ich hit þonke þe,   475
Nou þe eleue sterren icomen beþ to me.
Mi fader 7 mi moder haddich iwonne,
Þenne hadde ich iwis þe mone 7 þe sunne.
Feire beþ þis ȝunge men iserued þilke niȝt,
Of mete ne of drinke trukede hem no wiȝt.   480
Iosep cam to þe bord, anon he hem tolde
'Ich am,' he seide, 'Iosep, into Egipte þat ȝe solde.'
7 so he geþ to boure riȝt from þe bord,
7 wepeþ for blisse þat he ne mai speken a word.
Þenne seide Ruben, 'Ne seidich ȝou inouȝ,   485
To sungen on þat child þat ȝe hadden wouȝ.
Nolde ȝe me ileue ȝoure neuer on,   [f. 10]
Nou is icome þe time þat we beþ alle agon.'
Iosep cam into halle 7 sauȝ his breþren wepe,
He kisseþ Beniamin anon, his neb he gan wipe,   490·
7 so he goþ bi rewe 7 kusseþ hem eueruchon,
Seþþe he cam into Egypte nas he so bliþe man.

Þenne seide Iosep to his breþren anon,
' Þe sweuene þat me mette, ȝit nis hit nouȝt agon.
Ac ase ȝe wolleþ, breþren, þat ich be aliue,   495
Ȝe ssule fecchen oure fader 7 maken him ful bliþe,
7 oure kun alle 7 oure nextfolde,
Þat ich mowe in þis lond here lif holde.
For þe hunger haþ ibe two ȝer swiþe strong,
7 ȝit hit lasteþ fiue, 7 þat is al to long.'   500
Feire he ssrudde his breþren mid dereworþe cloþ,
His breþren þat rideþ 7 here men þat goþ.
Of fiss 7 of flesse, of foules ibake,
He lette senden in cartes to his fader sake,
Cloþes of skarlet 7 of sabelin,   505
Of honi 7 of corn, of fruit 7 of win,
Nappes of seluer 7 ringes of golde,
7 alle prudene mest þat hi leden wolde.
Feire fareþ þis ȝunge men bi dai 7 bi niȝt
To here fader Iacob þat hi comen riȝt.   510
7 habbeþ to Iacob ibrouȝt al þis þing,
7 seggeþ þat Iosep is in Egipte ase heiȝ as a king.
Þo Iacob iherde þat Iosep was aliue,
Nas neuere for his child fader so bliþe.   [f. 10b]
He caste awei his crucche, his mantel he feng,   515
Feire he platte his her wiþ a selkene streng.
He toc his benetene hat wiþ pal þat was biweued.
' Of sor 7 of serewe nou ich am bireued,
For nou me þuncheþ þat ich mai flen as an ern
For þe loue of Iosep, mi leueste bern.'   520
Iacob rod singinde, such hit were a child,
' For þe loue of Iosep nou ich am ȝung 7 wild.'
Þo Iosep iherde of his fader come,
Kniȝtes inowe mid him he haþ inome,

Mid harpe 7 mid pipe, mid ioie 7 mid songe　　　525
Mid alle worssipe mest his fader to vnderfonge.
Ic*h* ʒou mai telle 7 ic*h* ʒou mai singe
Þ*at* bliþe was Pharaon of Ioseppes þi*n*ge.
7 lond swiþe riche bi þe seeside
He haþ to Iacob iʒiue 7 castles heye 7 wide.　　　530
Nou haueþ Iacob wele 7 alle wi*n*ne
Mid his sones twolue 7 mid his oþer ku*n*ne.
Þe blisse is ful swete þ*at* comeþ after wo,
Wel is hi*m* a liue þ*at* his care mot <u>atgo</u>.
Nou þu*n*cheþ Iacob his lif swiþe swete　　　535
Of Iacob to telle nou ic*h* mot nede lete.
Come neu*er*e to þis hous worse tidinge
Bote alle worssipe mest 7 C*r*istes blessinge.　　Amen.

Explicit Iacob 7 Iosep [1].

[1] After *Iosep* an *h* has been erased.

NOTES

6. *to þe nale* for *to þen ale*, 'to the ale or ale-house'. The *þen* is dative: OE. *þǣm*. Cp. 29 *þe nendinge*; 327 *atte nende*. Cp. also Chaucer, *Freres Tale* 51 *And make him grete festes atte nale*.

7. *vcchen*, 'to increase, enlarge, distend': OWS. *īecan*, LWS. *ȳcan*.

10. *Bote we hit bileuen*, 'unless we give it up'.

12. *ligge slepe*, 'to lie sleeping'. *Slepe* is infinitive. Cp. *Cursor Mundi* 14172, *He lijs to dei*, 'He lies dying'.

such hit were a gris, 'as though it were a pig'. Cp. 371 *such hit were a king*, 382 *such hit were his gome*, 521 *such hit were a child*.

18. *riued*, adv. 'in great numbers'. It is formed, with irregular ending, from *rive*, obsolete form of *rife*.

pulle. Pull, 'a pool'. This word occurs in the OE. charters as *pull*, the form here, and *pyll*, whence apparently the sixteenth century *pill*.

29. *þe nendinge = þen endinge*. Cp. note to l. 6.

31. *þe elde man*. Cp. 169, 335 and *Havelok* 546 *an eld cloth*, 2472 *þe helde men*. For further instances of *eld*, 'old', cp. the β forms in N.E.D. s.v. *old*.

43. 'And as we reaped our corn.' I take *so* here in the sense of 'as, whilst, when'. The N.E.D. records no ME. instance of *so* with temporal meaning, but as it is used in this sense in OE. (e.g. *Genesis* 552, *Psalms* ed. Thorpe 113³) there seems to be no objection to assigning this meaning to it here.

62. *binime*, properly 'to take away'. Here it seems to mean 'to prevent'.

77. *woder*, 'whither'. The *o* (= *u*) is due to the influence of the *w*. Cp. § 5, 13.

92. *al an oþer*, adv. 'altogether differently'. Cp. *Havelok* 1395 *But auelok þouthe al anoþer*, and N.E.D. s.v. *another* adv.

94. *frome*, properly 'beginning'. It is here practically meaningless and added for the sake of the rhyme. Cp. 111, 117.

98. *beþ*, we should no doubt alter to *biþ*, as *beþ* otherwise only occurs in the pl.

100. *fotsid*, 'reaching down to the feet'. OE. *fōtsīd*. Cp. Napier, *Contributions to OE. Lexicography*, 1906, s.vv. *fōtsīd* and *lendensīd*, 'reaching to the loins'. The only instance in the N.E.D. is from Douglas, *Æneis* VII. xi. 31 *Gyrd in a garmont semely and futsyd*.

106. *hete* means probably not 'heat', but 'hatred, strife'. Cp. note to 316.

110. *A wey*, 'Alas'.

114. *of fer 7 of gris*. Cp. 208. The regular ME. form of *fer* is *veir*, 'a kind of fur'. OE. initial *f* had become *v* in the dialect of this poem, though generally written *f*, so that *fer* could stand for either *fer* or *ver*. The phrase *veir and gris* is common in ME. (cp. *Sir Tristrem* 1381, Mannyng's *Chronicle* 615, *Cursor Mundi* 25466; etc.) and is from the O. French *vair et gris*.

116. *Egipte* is gen. pl., OE. *Egypta*, 'of the Egyptians'. In l. 143 we get the weak gen. *Egiptene*.

118. *come*. May not the original have had *comeþ* and a later copyist have altered to *come* for the sake of the rhyme? Cp. § 8.

133. *panes*, 'pence', is from the form *panig*, which appears in the twelfth century by the side of the regular *penig*.

135. Is the form *fengeþ* miswritten for *fongeþ*?

136. *Darf no man axe*, 'No one need ask'. *Darf = þarf*. Forms with initial *d* for *þ* occur elsewhere in the case of this verb: in *Moral Ode* 43 two MSS. read *darf*, whilst the remaining five have initial *þ*; in *King Horn* 388 MS. C has *dorte* for *þorte*. Cp. also N.E.D. s.v. *þarf*.

143. *Egiptene*, gen. pl. Cp. note to 116.

164–5. The poet is evidently thinking of only one of the two chapmen.

177. *a liue*, 'in my life, all my life'.

178. *be* is 1st person pres. indic. with future meaning, 'I shall never be blithe'. Cp. 349, 462. Cp. also *Laȝamon* 28218 *ne beo ich nauere bliðe*.

199. After this line a line has been lost, as the rhyme shows.

203. 'What may your will be?'

215. The original probably had *werned* with inexact rhyme :
cp. 390–1 *bringe* : *vingres*.

233. *þeiȝ he ne hadde grome.* For *ne hadde* one would expect
hadde (*þeiȝ he hadde grome*). For the use of OE. *þēah*, ME.
þeiȝ = 'if, even if' in sentences beginning with ' It is no wonder',
cp. Koch, *Historische Gramm. der engl. Sprache* (ed. Zupitza), ii.
459, and N.E.D. s.v. *though*, II, 4.

264. *arouȝt.* One would expect *arauȝt* from OE. *areaht.* It is
probably merely a scribal error.

267. *holen out,* ' hollow out, pick out'. It is infin. governed
by *ssulen,* to be supplied from the preceding *ssalt.*

278. *riȝtwis* refers to *Louerd.*

284. Cp. § 5, 12.

291. *vrles.* Cp. § 5, 4.

293. *aiwiȝt,* ' at all, in any way '. It stands for *aniwiht,* the
ai being the contraction for *ani* found in the South in the twelfth
and thirteenth centuries.

303. *7 quite faten of bende.* *Faren* was apparently first
written and then altered by the scribe to *faten.* What this
means I do not know and prefer to read *7 quite of bende,* 'and
release from his bonds '.

316. *hunger 7 hete.* This phrase occurs elsewhere ; it is
frequent in *Laȝamon* (4042 &c.), and I take *hete* to mean ' hatred,
enmity', rather than ' heat'. Cp. Madden's note in his
Laȝamon, iii, p. 464. It also occurs in *St. Katherine* 2401. In
this phrase *hete* has of course lost its original meaning, and the
whole implies ' want and trouble.'

317. Read *drinke.* The *n* may have been added, for metrical
reasons, before the following vowel.

324. After this line a leaf has been cut out.

330. *Ofte of þis smal chaf þis breþren brouȝten hom.* This
I take it is a reference to the chaff story mentioned on p. xii, which
was probably told on the lost leaf.

334. *nadda = nadde heo,* ' she had not '.

327. *atte nende = atten ende.* Cp. note to l. 6.

360. *arugge,* ' on (his) back '. OE. *on hrycge.*

363. *tubrugge.* The OE. form, which is not recorded, would be
tygebrycg.

364. For the *parle* of the MS. we must obviously read *þar þe.*

369. *let* for *lete* (pret. subj.) for the sake of the rhyme.

381. *For muchel one nede,* 'for a great need'. For the position of the article cp. '*many (such) a need*'.

384. *heiȝte,* 'is called'.

391. *halde,* 'poured': OWS. *hieldan,* Angl. *hældan.* Cp. *Laȝamon* 1196 *He halde þa milc in þat fur,* 14995 *þat atter heo halde in þat win.* Cp. also N.E.D. s.v. *hield.*

401. *was Pharaones þe king.* When two possessive genitives stand in apposition, the second has in ME. no inflexion. The two genitives are generally separated by the governing substantive as in l. 416 *Of Faraones lond þe king.* This construction is very common in ME., e.g. Chaucer, *Book of the Duchess* 282 *The kinges meting Pharao,* 'the dream of king Pharao'.

402. *wiþinne þe prene.* Can a wooden skewer be here meant with which the sack was fastened? The meaning would be that the cup was put at the top of the sack, just under the fastening.

403. *come.* The *pl.* form instead of the correct *cam* owing to the following *þis ȝunge men.*

407. *twolf.* Cp. 532 *twolue* and § 5, 13.

410–12. Note that these three lines rhyme.

416. Cp. 401.

418. *drem,* 'loud lamentation'. Cp. *Beues of Hamtoun,* ed. Kölbing, 1339 *Saber wep and made drem.*

434. For instances of *no* = 'nor' cp. N.E.D. s.v. *no,* conj.

455. MS. *hise ten breþren.* This cannot be right. Read *þis ten breþren* or *hise ten sones* (?)

464. *awreke,* properly 'to avenge'. Can it be here 'make good my loss, comfort'?

486. *sungen,* OE. *syngian,* 'to sin'. Cp. Ekwall, *ESt.* 40, 161 ff. According to Ekwall 'the *g* forms in this and similar cases only occur in writings which belong to the middle or western portions of the south, or the southern part of the west midland area.'

487. *ȝoure neuer on,* 'never one of you'.

497. *oure kun alle 7 oure nextfolde,* 'all our kin and our most intimate friends'. *Nextfolde* here used as sb. It is properly an adj., cp. *Juliana* p. 32, *Al mi nestfalde cun.* Cp. OE. *nēah-*

feald, 'intimate' (not in the dictionaries) as in *to his nēah-fealdum frēondum*, and *nēahfealdlīc* (Napier, *Contributions to OE. Lexicography*, p. 47).

502. *goþ*, 'go on foot, walk'.

517. *benetene*, so MS. I have left it in the text, but it is clearly miswritten for *beuerene*, 'made of beaver skin, for the confusion of *t* and *r* is common in MSS. of this period. The only two instances of *beveren* in the N.E.D. mean 'beaver coloured', but there is no reason why it should not be used in the sense of 'made of beaver skin'. Cp. Chaucer, *Prol.* 272 *Upon his heed a Flaundrish bever hat'*.

522. *wild* for *wilde* on account of the rhyme.

523. *come*, 'coming'. The *o* of course = *u* and is due to the influence of the verb ; OE. *cyme* would have yielded ME. *cüme*.

GLOSSARY

a, an, *indef. art.* a, an, 10, 12, 35, 47 ...

a-, *prep.* weakened from *on* in adverbial expressions such as: afelde, a līue, aknē, aniȝt, q.v.

ā, *exclamation*, ah, alas! 110, 227, 459.

abīden, *str. vb.* I. to stop, abide, endure; *inf.* abīde, 244; *imp. pl.* abīdeþ, 410.

aboute, *adv.* about, round, 453.

ac, *conj.* but, 64, 81, 94, 103 ...

adoun, *adv.* down, to the ground, 175, 458.

afēld(e), *adv.* afield, in the fields, to the fields, 41, 63, 69, 347 ...

afēldward, *adv.* towards the fields, 73.

afingred, *adj.* starved, hungry, 333. [OE. *ofhyngred.*]

after, *prep.* after, next to, 2, 196, 207, 263 ...

aȝein, *adv.* again, back again, 299, 411, 417, 419 ...

agōn, *anom. vb.* to go to ruin, to be fulfilled; *p.p.* agōn, 319, 488, gone to ruin; 494, fulfilled.

aiwiȝt, *adv.* at all, 293 (note).

aknē, *adv.* on (one's) knees, 375; aknē sitten, to kneel, 67, 376.

al,[1] *pl.* alle *adj.* all, 32, 45, 61, 86 ...

al,[2] *adv.* entirely, completely, 102, 171, 173, 261 ...; al an ōþer, altogether differently, 92.

aldren, *sb. pl.* forefathers, 13.

āle, *sb.* ale, ale-house; þe nāle = þen āle, 6.

alīue,[1] *adj.* alive, 213, 348, 364, 386 ...

a līue,[2] *adv.* in (one's) life, 177, 321, 534.

al ōne, *adv.* quite alone, 76.

alōnged, *adj.* filled with longing, 389, 474.

alsō,[1] *adv.* as, thus, to this degree, in the same manner, 272, 387; ase, 60, 195, 240.

alsō,[2] *conj.* as, while, 84; ase, 41, 137, 219, 262 ...

am, see bēn.

amorewen, *adv.* on the morrow, 262, 290.

āngel, *sb.* angel, 156.

anhōn, *str. vb. redup.* to hang; *p.p.* anhōnge, 414.

anhōnge, see anhōn.

anhōngen, *wk. vb.* to hang; *p.p.* anhōnged, 266.

aniȝt, *adv.* in the night, 35.

anōn, *adv.* forthwith, at once, 92, 163, 296, 421 ...

aquellen, *wk. vb.* to kill; *pres. ind. pl.* aquelleþ, 98.

arecchen, *wk. vb.* to expound, explain; *p.p.* arouȝt, 264 (note).

arēden, *str. vb. redup.* to interpret; *inf.* arēde, 120; *imp. sg.* arēd, 52.

arīsen, *str. vb.* I. to arise; *imp. pl.* arīseþ, 376.

arm, *sb.* arm, 222.

arouȝt, see arecchen.

art, artōu, see bēn.

aruȝ, *adj.* bad, evil, 198. [OE. *earg.*]

arügge, *adv.* on (his) back, 360.

ase, *adv.* and *conj.*, see alsō.

assen *sb.* (*pl.* of ass), asses, 114, 344, 362, 398 ...

astōnden, *str. vb.* VI. to withstand, oppose; *inf.* astōnde, 211.

at, *prep.* at, 64, 67 ... at ōn, agreed, 131. Cp. atte. .

atgǭn, *anom. vb.* to escape from ;
  inf. atgǭ, 534.

athǫlden, *str. vb. redup.* to keep
  hold of ; *pret. sg.* athŭld, 223
  (cp. § 5, 9).

atte = at þe, at the, 94, 104, 111,
  117 ...

awarien, *wk. vb.* to curse ; *p.p.*
  awaried (accurst), 427.

awǣken, *str. vb.* VI. to awaken ;
  pret. sg. awōc, 290.

awei, *adv.* away, 515.

awrēken, *str. vb.* V. to comfort (?) ;
  inf. awrēke, 464 (note).

axen, *wk. vb.* to ask ; *inf.* axe,
  136 ; *pres. ind. sg.* axeþ, 68 ; —
  pl. axeþ, 123 ; *pret. sg.* axede,
  77, 165.

bachŭs, *sb.* bakehouse, 259.

bāken, *str. vb.* VI. to bake ; *p.p.*
  ibāke, 503.

bāle, *sb.* misery, death, 98.

barǭn, *sb.* baron, 291, 292.

basket, *sb.* basket, 260.

baxtere, *sb.* baker, 248, 258, 266,
  297.

bēden, *str. vb.* II. to offer ; *pres.
  ind. pl.* bēdeþ, 131.

beggen, see bŭggen.

bēme, *sb.* trumpet, 230.

bēn, *anom. vb.* to be ; *inf.* bē(n),
  52, 55, 104 ... ; *pres. ind.* I. *sg.*
  am, 217, 482, 518 ... ; bē (with
  future meaning), 178 (note), 349,
  462 ... ; — 2. *sg.* art, 204 ; artóu
  (= art þóu), 459 ; —3. *sg.* is, 6, 9,
  ... ; biþ (with fut. meaning), 10 ;
  bēþ, 98 (note) ; — *pl.* bēþ, 80,
  123, 129 ... ; bē ȝe, 361 ; *pres.
  subj.* bē, 68, 70, 123 ... ; *pret.
  sg.* was, 4, 59 ... ; — *pl.* wēre(n),
  15, 17, 81 ... ; *subj. sg.* and *pl.*
  wēre, 12, 41, 52 ... ; *p.p.* ibē, 499.
  With negation : *pres. ind.* 3. *sg.*
  nis, 199, 213 ; *pret. sg.* nas, 19,
  174, 218 ; — *pl.* nēre, 289.

bēnd, *sb.* bond, fetter, 299, 303.

bēnden, *wk. vb.* to bend ; *p.p.*
  ibent, 194.

beneten, MS., see bēueren.

bēren, *str. vb.* IV. to bear, carry ;
  in *p.p.* born ; *inf.* bēre, 87,
  260 ; *pret. sg.* bar, 360 ; bēr
  (clēr), 256 ; — (frē)bǫren, 366.

berewen, *str. vb.* III. to guard,
  protect ; *pres. subj. sg.* berewe,
  72, 351.

bērn,¹ *sb.* barn, 357.

bērn,² *sb.* child, 520.

bēten, *wk. vb.* to atone for, make
  good ; *pret. sg.* bette, 201.

betere, *adj.* (comp. of gōd), better,
  28, 342.

bēþ, see bēn.

bēueren, *adj.* made of beaver skin,
  517 (note). (MS. benetene, read
  beuerene).

bi, *prep.* in, during (of time), by,
  beside, 13, 18, 24, 81 ... ; bi þe
  lifte, in the air, 261, 267.

bicǫmen, *str. vb.* IV. to fit, suit,
  come to pass ; *pret. sg.* bicam,
  100, 272.

bidden, *str. vb.* V. (1) to beg, ask ;
  pres. ind. sg. bidde, 361 ; *pret.
  sg.* bad, 36, 219, 240, 332 ... ;
  (2) to bid, 311.

bīden, *str. vb.* I. to endure ; *pres.
  subj. sg.* bīde, 239.

bihǫlden, *str. vb. redup.* to behold ;
  inf. bihǫlde, 152, 172 ; *pres.
  ind.* 3. *sg.* bihalt, 33 ; — *pl.*
  bihǫldeþ, 129 ; *pret. sg.* bihŭld
  (on), looked on, 161 (cp. § 5,
  9).

bihǫten, *str. vb. redup.* to promise ; *pret. sg.* bihēt, 22, 368.

bifǫre(n), *prep.* before, 301, 367.

biginnen, *str. vb.* III. to begin ;
  pret. sg. bigan, 34.

bilēuen, *wk. vb.* (1) to abandon,
  give up ; *pres. subj. pl.* bilēuen,
  10 ; (2) to remain ; *inf.* bilēue,
  346 ; *p.p.* bilēued, 348.

bimēnen, *wk. vb.* to bemoan; *inf.* bimēne, 305.

bīnden, *str. vb.* III. to bind; *inf.* bīnde, 234.

binimen, *str. vb.* IV. to prevent; *inf.* binime, 62 (note).

birēuen, *wk. vb.* to free from; *p.p.* birēued, 518.

bisēchen, *wk. vb.* to beseech, beg for; *p.p.* bisouȝt, 450.

bisīdes, *adv.* close by, near, 95, 105, 112.

bisouȝt, see bisēchen.

bistēken, *str. vb.* V. to shut up, imprison; *p.p.* bistēke, 220, 295.

bitēchen, *wk. vb.* to entrust; *pres. ind. sg.* bitēcheþ, 470.

bitīden, *wk. vb.* to betide, happen; *pres. subj.* 54, 55, 245.

bitwēne, *prep.* between, 110; hem bitwēne, to one another, 88.

biþ, see bēn.

biwēuen, *wk. vb.* to clothe, cover; *p.p.* biwēued, 425, 517.

blessinge, *sb.* blessing, 444, 538.

blisse, *sb.* joy, happiness, pleasure, 149, 251, 275, 309 ...

blīþe, *adj.* pleased, glad, 33, 139, 178, 212 ...; *comp.* blīþore, 472.

blōc, *adj.* pale, 304.

blōd, *sb.* blood, 96, 173.

blōdi, *adj.* bloodstained, 171.

blōwen, *str. vb. redup.* to blow; *pres. part.* blōwinde, 230.

bōc, *sb.* book, 184.

bōld, *adj.* bold, brave, 151, 291.

bōrd, *sb.* table, 191, 262, 481, 483.

bōte, *conj.* (1) but, 4, 538; (2) unless (with *subj.*), 10, 319.

bōtiler, *sb.* butler, cup-bearer, 247, 254, 268, 273, 294.

bōur, *sb.* bower, 147, 153, 202, 205 ...

bōwe, *sb.* bow, 194.

brēd, *sb.* bread, 260, 332, 334.

breiden, *str. vb.* III. to tear off (a garment); *pret. sg.* braid, 224.

brēken, *str. vb.* IV. to break, transgress; *pres. subj. pl.* brēke, 463; *pret. sg.* brac, 200.

brēþren, see brōþer.

briȝt, *adj.* bright, 148.

bringen, *anom. vb.* to bring; *inf.* bringe, 301, 363, 390 ...; *pres. ind. sg.* bringeþ, 428; — *pl.* bringeþ, 171; *imp. sg.* bring, 71; *pret. sg.* brouȝtem = brouȝte hem, 368; — *pl.* brouȝten, 330; *p.p.* ibrouȝt, 140, 265, 419 ...

brōd, *adj.* broad, wide, 283.

brōþer (*pl.* brēþren), *sb.* brother, *sg.* 94, 103; *pl.* 42, 57, 59, 61 ...

brūnie, *sb.* corselet, armour, 408.

bǔġġen, beġġen, *wk. vb.* to buy; *inf.* bǔġġen, 345; — beġġe, 130, 362; *pret. sg.* bouȝte, 164; *p.p.* ibouȝt, 139.

burȝ, *sb.* town, city, 145, 149.

burġeis, *sb.* citizen, burgess; *pl.* burġeis, 151, 291.

canst, *anom. vb.* art able; *pres. ind.* 2. *sg.* canst, 214; *pret. sg.* cóuþe (knew, was able), 143, 293, 323.

cāre, *sb.* care, harm, 72, 167, 351, 534.

cart, *sb.* cart, waggon, 504.

castel, *sb.* castle, 368, 370, 469; *pl.* castles, 146, 530.

casten, *wk. vb.* to cast, to put (hand in purse); *inf.* casten, 133, 163; *pret. sg.* caste, 515; *p.p.* icast, 249.

chaf, *sb.* chaff, 330.

chapman, *sb.* merchant, 112, 118, 121, 129 ...; chapmon, 164.

chēpen, *wk. vb.* to offer (for sale), bargain; *pres. ind. pl.* chēpeþ, 131; *pret. pl.* chēpeden, 122.

child, *sb.* child, 66, 67, 76 77 ...

chin, *sb.* chin, 101.

clēpen, *wk. vb.* to call; *pres. ind.*

sg. clẹ̄peþ, 65 ; *pret. sg.* clẹ̄-
pede, 339.
clẹ̄r, *adj.* clear, pure, 257.
clọ̄þ, *sb.* cloth, garment, 501, 505.
clüppen, *wk. vb.* to embrace; *inf.*
clüppe, 216.
cofre, *sb.* coffer, 163.
cȯme, *sb.* coming, arrival, 523.
cȯmen, *str. vb.* IV. to come ; *inf.*
cȯme(n), 8, 54, 58, 112 ... ;
pres. ind. 3. *sg.* cȯmeþ, 88, 533 ;
— *pl.* cȯmeþ, 32, 170 ; cȯme
(see note), 118 ; *pres. subj. sg.*
cȯme, 537 ; *imp. pl.* cȯmeþ,
124 ; *pret. sg.* cam, 87, 91, 202,
230 ... ; cōme (see note), 403 ;
— *pl.* cōme(n), 113, 121, 151,
225 ... ; *p.p.* icȯme(n), 66, 156,
159, 378 ...
cȯntre, *sb.* country, 405.
corn, *sb.* corn, 43, 341, 345, 362 ...
cȯupe, *sb.* cup, 256.
cȯupe, see canst.
crücche, *sb.* crutch, 515.
cürtel, see kürtel.

dai, *sb.* day, 193, 239, 246, 265 ... ;
dat. pl. dawe [= OE. *dagum*],
13.
darf, see þarf.
dawe, see dai.
day(e), see dai.
dẹ̄d, *adj.* dead, 253, 277, 333, 373.
dẹ̄men, *wk. vb.* to adjudge ; *p.p.*
idẹ̄med, 414.
dẹ̄p, *adj.* deep, 95.
dẹ̄r, *sb.* beast, wild beast, 180.
dẹ̄re, *adj.* dear, beloved, 37.
dẹ̄rewȯrþe, *adj.* precious, valu-
able, costly, 187, 501 ; *super.*
dẹ̄rewȯrþest, 201.
dẹrne, *adv.* secretly, 214.
dẹ̄þ, *sb.* death, 86, 459.
deyen, *wk.vb.* to die; *inf.* deye, 343.
dich, *sb.* dyke, ditch, 18.
dōm, *sb.* fate, sentence, 414, 443.
dōn, *anom. vb.* to do, to cast (into
bonds, &c.) ; *inf.* dō(n), 219,

321 ; *imp. sg.* dȯ, 37, 299 ; *pret.*
sg. and *pl.* düde, 24, 242, 400 ;
p.p. idȯ, 62, 229, 240.
drawen, *str. vb.* VI. to draw; *inf.*
drawen, 111 ; *pret. pl.* drōwen,
127. Cp. ȯutdrawen.
drẹ̄m, *sb.* loud lamentation, 418
(note).
drẹ̄ri, *adj.* sad, gloomy, 418.
drinc, *sb.* drink, 14, 359, 393,
480... ; drinken, 317 (note).
drinken, *str. vb.* III. to drink ;
inf. drinke, 17, 28 ; *pret. sg.*
dranc, 445.
drinken, *sb.* see drinc.
drïuen, *str. vb.* I. to drive ; *inf.*
drïue, 327.
düde, see dōn.
durste, *anom. vb. pret. sg.* dared,
305.

Ebrewiss, *adj.* Hebrew, 227, 395.
Egipte,[1] *sb.* the Egyptians ; *gen. pl.*
Egipte lọ̄nd, land of the
Egyptians, Egypt, 116 (note),
119, 142, 158 ... ; *gen. pl.*
Egiptene, 143.
Egipte,[2] *sb.* Egypt, 215, 319,
329 ...
ẹ̄k, *adv.* also, as well, 57.
ẹ̄ld, *adj.* old, 31 (note), 169, 335.
See ọ̄ld.
elleue, *numeral,* eleven, 50, 476 ;
elleuene, 436, 471.
em, see hem.
ẹ̄nde, *sb.* end, 298, 302; atte
nẹ̄nde of lọ̄nd, out of the
country, 327.
ẹ̄ndinge, *sb.* ending, end ; þe
nẹ̄ndinge = þen ẹ̄ndinge, 29.
ẹ̄ni, *adj.* any, 148.
ẹ̄r,[1] *adv.* previously, before, 21,
81, 452.
ẹ̄r(e),[2] *prep.* before, ere, 405 ; ẹ̄r
þis, before now, 95.
ẹ̄rest, *adv.* (super. of ẹ̄r), first, 427.
ẹ̄rliche, *adv.* early, 8.
ẹ̄rn, *sb.* eagle, 519.

ẹrnde, *sb.* message, errand ; þat
tẹrnde = þat þe ẹrnde, 87.

ẹrnen, *wk. vb.* to earn ; *inf.* ẹrne,
342.

ẹror, *adv.* (comp. of ẹr) earlier,
formerly, 450.

ẹstẹnde, *sb.* East country, 341.

ẹþ, *adj.* easy, 120, 312.

ẹuel, *sb.* evil, 73.

ẹuer(e), *adv.* ever, continually,
137, 177, 179, 200 ...

ẹuerüchọn, *pron.* every one, 91,
287, 339, 422 ...

eye, *sb.* eye, 267.

fader, *sb.* father, 24, 35, 47,
49 ... ; vader, 39.

fain, *adv.* eagerly, fain, 78, 441.

fallen, *str. vb. redup.* to fall,
happen ; *inf.* falle, 46 ; *pres.
ind.* 3. *sg.* falleþ, 466 ; — *pl.*
valleþ, 375 ; *pret. sg.* fel, 175,
193, 231, 254 ... ; — *pl.* fellen,
48, 50 ; *p.p.* ifalle, 455.

fāren, *str. vb.* VI. (1) to go, travel,
fare ; *inf.* fāren, 438 ; *pres. ind.
pl.* fāreþ, 352, 416, 447, 467, 509 ;
pres. subj. sg. fāre, 168 ; — *pl.*
fāre, 71.

faste, *adv.* firmly, securely, 234.

fat, *adj.* fat, 284, 285, 287, 288.

fẹ, *sb.* cattle, money, 63, 135.

fecchen, *wk. vb.* to fetch ; *inf.*
496 ; *pres. ind. sg.* feccheþ, 304.

feir, *adj.* fair, handsome, pleasant,
5, 125, 147, 189 ...

feire, *adv.* fairly, graciously,
honourably, 25, 44, 68, 166 ...

fẹld, *sb.* field, 32, 44, 80, 170 ...

fẹle, *adj.* many, 225.

fellen, *wk. vb.* to fell, lay low,
humble ; *inf.* felle, 313.

fẹngeþ, see fọngen.

fer, *adv.* far, far away, 119.

fẹr, *sb.* kind of fur, 114 (note),
208.

fērāde, *sb.* train, following, 160.
[OE. *gefērrǣden.*]

fēren, *wk. vb.* to live, behave, to
go (one's way) ; *pret. plur.*
fērden, 13, 406.

ferren, *adj.* having come from far,
366.

fẹt, see fọt.

fif, *numeral,* five ; *inflected* fiue,
500.

fīn, *adj.* of fīne nẹde, of absolute
necessity, 58.

fīnden, *str. vb.* III. to find, devise ;
inf. fīnde(n), 75, 82, 83 ... ;
pret. sg. fọnd, 76 ; fünde, 427 ;
— *pl.* fünden, 359 ; *p.p.* ifünde,
421.

finger, *sb.* finger, 222 ; vingres,
391.

fiue, see fif.

fiss, *sb.* fish, 503.

flẹn, *str. vb.* III. to fly ; *inf.* flẹn,
519.

flẹten, *str. vb.* II. to float ; *pret.
pl.* flọten, 18.

flẹss, *sb.* flesh, meat, 503.

flọd, *sb.* flood, 2, 3, 16, 20.

flọur, *sb.* flower, 148.

fọ, *sb.* foe, 60 ; *pl.* fọn, 74.

fọn, *str. vb. redup.* to begin ; *inf.*
fọn (on), 21 ; *pres. ind. pl.*
fọþ (on), 105 ; *pret. sg.* fẹng,
176, 224, 231, 254. Cp. fọngen.

fọngen, *str. vb. redup.* to take,
seize, catch ; *inf.* fọnge, 459 ;
pres. ind. pl. fẹngeþ (for
fọngeþ (?), 135 (note) ; *pret. sg.*
fẹng, 425, 515 ; *p.p.* ifọnge,
413. Cp. fọn.

for,[1] *conj.* for, 29, 137, 309.

for,[2] *prep.* by reason of, for, in
exchange for, 15, 58, 104, 128 ...

forʒiuen, *str. vb.* V. to pardon ;
pres. ind. 1. *sg.* forʒiue, 303.

forlẹten, *str. vb. redup.* to leave ;
pres. ind. 3. *sg.* forlẹteþ, 138.

forswolewen, *str. vb.* III. to
swallow up ; *p.p.* forswolewed,
288.

for tō, *prep.* with *inf.* in order to, also merely equivalent to *to* with *inf.* 28, 97, 150, 182 ...

forþ, *adv.* forth, out, 304, 465.

for þī, *adv.* therefore, on this account, 16, 144.

fōt (*pl.* fēt), *sb.* foot ; *sg.* 48, 50, 67, 455 ... ; *pl.* 46, 58, 231, 375 ...

fōtsīd, *adj.* reaching down to the feet, 100 (note).

foul, *sb.* fowl, bird, 261, 267, 503.

frē, *adj.* frank, straightforward, 64, 202 ; freeborn, highborn, 153.

frēbǭren, *adj.* freeborn, 366.

fremede, *adj.* not akin, 181, 252, 276.

frēnd, *sb.* friend, 235, 454.

frēten, *str. vb.* V. to devour ; *pret. pl.* frēte, 287.

from, *prep.* from, 32, 72, 156, 167 ... ; vrom, 113.

frōme, *sb.* beginning ; atte frōme, at first, first, 94 (note), 111, 117.

fruit, *sb.* fruit, 506.

ful,[1] *adj.* full, complete, absolute, 17, 60, 74, 257 ; *comp.* fullore, 289.

ful,[2] *adv.* very, 8, 9, 59, 107 ...

füllen, *wk. vb.* to fill ; *inf.* füllen, 11 ; *pret. sg.* fülde, 260 ; — *pl.* fülden, 14.

fullore, see ful.

fürst, *adv.* first, for the first time, 295.

gāme, gamen, *sb.* sport, game, pursuit, pleasure, 5, 10, 108 ; gǭme, 228, 329, 354, 382.

gan, *aux. vb. str.* III. did ; *pret. sg.* gan, 172, 216, 255, 325 ... ; — *pl.* gǒnne(n), 46, 60, 261, 286.

gēþ, see gǭn.

gistnien, *wk. vb.* to lodge, entertain ; *inf.* gistni, 365.

glad, *adj.* glad, 218, 241, 397, 451.

gladien, gladen, *wk. vb.* to

comfort, cheer ; *inf.* gladien, 434 ; gladen, 182, 432.

god, *sb.* God, 23, 37, 47, 167 ...

gōd, *adj.* good, 1, 85, 108, 128 ...

gōld, *sb.* gold, 163, 209, 345, 415.

gǭme, see gāme.

gǒn, *anom. vb.* to go, to walk ; *inf.* gǭ(n), 6, 76, 284, 286 ; *pres. ind.* 3. *sg.* gēþ, 73, 85, 483 ; gǭþ, 388, 473, 491 ; — *pl.* gǭþ, 502 ; *imp. sg.* gǭ, 82, 83 ; *p.p.* igǭ(n), 103, 297, 347, 381. Cp. also agǒn, and atgǭ.

gǒnne(n), see gan.

gǭþ, see gǒn.

grāme, *sb.* anger, wrath, 3 ; grǭme, 233.

grāpe, *sb.* grape, 257.

grēden, *wk. vb.* to cry out, mourn ; *pres. ind. sg.* grēdeþ, 466.

grēne, *adj.* green, 283.

grēt, *adj.* great, large, 115.

grēten, *wk. vb.* to greet ; *pret. sg.* grettem = grette hem, 91.

grīpen, *str. vb.* I. to seize ; *pres. ind. pl.* grīpeþ, 92.

grīs,[1] *sb.* young pig, 12.

grīs,[2] *sb.* grey fur, 114, 208.

grǭme, see grāme.

gründ, *sb.* destruction, ruin ; to þe gründe bringen = to ruin, 428.

gülden, *adj.* golden, 401, 412.

gült, *sb.* guilt, 303.

gülteles, *adj.* guiltless, 242, 243, 428.

gürdel, *sb.* girdle, 7.

ȝē, yea, yes, 431.

ȝē, *pers. pron.* 2. *pl. nom.* ye, you, 1, 124, 265, 340 ...

ȝēme, *sb.* heed, care ; ȝēme nimen, to take heed, trouble oneself about, look after, 225, 273, 399.

ȝēr, *sb.* year, 246, 314, 499.

ȝērne, *adv.* eagerly, earnestly, 36.

ȝif, *conj.* if, 52, 82, 83, 98 ... ; if, 372.

ʒit, *adv.* yet, still, 47, 49, 54, 55 …;
   ʒüt, 56. Cp. § 5, 10.
ʒiuen, *str. vb.* V. to give ; *pres.
   ind.* 3. *sg.* ʒiueþ, 188 ; *pret. sg.*
   ʒaf, 99, 165 ; *p.p.* iʒiue, 530.
ʒiuernesse, *sb.* greediness, glut-
   tony, 15.
ʒóu, *pers. pron.* 2. *pl. acc.* and
   dat. you, 3, 342, 345, 351 … ;
   óu, 22.
ʒóure,¹ *poss. adj.* 2. *pl.* your, 45,
   342, 344, 350 …
ʒóure,² *pers. pron.* 2. *pl. gen.* of
   you, 487.
ʒung, *adj.* young, 34, 134, 138,
   252 …
ʒungling, *sb.* youth, lad, 144, 280,
   301.
ʒüt, see ʒit.

habben, *wk. vb.* to have ; *inf.*
   habbe(n), 62, 208, 228, 314;
   haue, 210, 316 ; *pres. ind.* 1.
   sg. haue, 205, 461 ; — 3. *sg.*
   haueþ, 264, 531 ; haþ, 450, 452,
   499, 524 … ; —*pl.* habbeþ, 86,
   93, 139, 140… ; habbe ʒe (we),
   430, 444 ; *pret. pl.* hadden, 182,
   486 ; *pret. subj. sg.* hadde,
   233, 348, 478 ; haddich, 477 ;
   heuede, 240. With negation :
   pres. ind. 1. *sg.* nabbi (I have
   not), 309 ; — 3. *sg.* naþ, 275,
   380 ; — *pl.* nabbeþ, 251 ; *pret.
   sg.* nadda (she had not), 334.
   Cp. § 11, i.
hadde(n), see habben.
haddich, see habben.
haf, see hebben.
halde, see hęlden.
halle, *sb.* hall, 31, 65, 147, 169 …
harpe, *sb.* harp, 251, 270, 275,
   360 …
hat, *sb.* hat, 517.
hātien, *wk. vb.* to hate ; *inf.*
   hātie, 60; *pret. pl.* hāteden, 61.
hatte, see hǫten.
haþ, haue(þ), see habben.

hē, *pers. pron.* 3. *sg. masc. nom.* he,
   25, 26, 27 …
hebben, *str. vb.* VI. to lift ; *pret.
   sg.* haf, 166.
heie, see heiʒ.
heiʒ, *adj.* high, 19, 125, 435, 512 ;
   pl. heie, 146 ; heye, 357, 530.
heiʒte, see hǫten.
hęlden, *wk. vb.* to pour ; *pret. sg.*
   halde, 391 (note).
helm, *sb.* helmet, 408.
help, *sb.* help, 280, 319.
helpen, *str. vb.* III. to help ; *inf.*
   helpe, 90, 97 ; *pres. subj. sg.*
   helpe, 134.
hem, *pers. pron.* 3. *pl. acc.* and
   dat. them ; *acc.* 44, 78, 82, 83 … ;
   brouʒtem, 368 ; grettem, 9,
   dat. 6, 33, 59, 81 …
hēnde, *adj.* pleasant, amiable,
   gracious, 64, 202, 279 ; *super.*
   hēndeste, 364.
hēo, *pers. pron.* 3. *sg. fem. nom.*
   she, 196, 216, 217, 223 …
hēr, *sb.* hair, 516.
here, *poss. adj.* 3. *pl.* their, 14,
   60, 63, 70 …
hēr(e), *adv.* here, 42, 88, 95,
   118 …
hēren, *wk. vb.* to hear ; *inf.* hēre,
   28 ; *pres. ind.* 3. *sg.* hēreþ,
   29 ; *pret. sg.* hērde, 30, 294.
   Cp. ihēren.
hęren, *wk. vb.* to praise ; *inf.*
   hęren, 278.
hēron, hereon, 320, 322.
heste,*sb.* command, behest, 38,211.
hęte, *sb.* hate, enmity, strife, 106,
   316 (note), 343.
hęued, *sb.* head, 426.
heuede, see habben.
heuen, *sb.* heaven, 72, 156, 435,
   472 …
heye, *adv.* high, 266.
hī, *pers. pron.* 3. *pl. nom.* they,
   14, 17, 18, 45 …
hider, *adv.* hither, 378, 381.
him, *pers. pron.* 3. *sg. masc. acc.*

and *dat.* him ; *acc.* 36, 68, 92, 93 ... ; *dat.* 35, 67, 75, 79 ...

hinderling, *sb.* mean person, wretch, 89.

hine, *pers. pron.* 3. *sg. masc. acc.* him, 61, 137, 242, 465.

hir, see hire.¹

hire,¹ *poss. adj.* 3. *sg. fem.* her, 176, 222, 224 ; **hir,** 195 (cp. § 11, iii).

hire,² *pers. pron.* 3. *sg. fem. dat.* her, 196.

his, *poss. adj.* 3. *sg. masc.* his, 4, 24, 25, 35 ... ; *pl.* **hise,** 86 (cp. § 11, iii).

hit, *pers. pron.* 3. *sg. neut. nom.* and *acc.* it ; *nom.* 10, 11, 12, 52 ... ; *acc.* 10, 47 ...

hǭlden, *str. vb. redup.* to protect, preserve ; *inf.* **hǭlde,** 498.

hǭlen, *wk. vb.* to hollow out, pick out ; *inf.* 267.

hǭm,¹ *sb.* home ; **at hǭm,** 64, 343, 346, 348 ...

hǭm,² *adv.* homewards, 32, 71, 170, 330 ...

hǭnd, *sb.* hand, 133, 141 ... ; *pl.* **hǭnde(n),** 109, 132, 185, 335 ...

hǒni, *sb.* honey, 506.

hǭr, *adj.* hoary, 175.

horn, *sb.* horn, 344.

hǭten, *str. vb. redup.* to call, name ; *p.p.* **ihǭten,** 113 ; *pres. ind.* 3. *sg. passive* **hatte** (is called), 80 ; **heiȝte** (is called), 384.

hǒu, *adv.* how, 168, 279, 280, 297 ... ; **hū,** 71.

hǒus, *sb.* house, 537.

hū, see hǒu.

hül, *sb.* hill, mountain, 19.

hunger, *sb.* hunger, famine, 316, 343, 454, 499 ... ; **on hunger dęd,** dead of hunger, 373.

i-, particle used with verbs, especially with *p.p.* ; see under simplex. [OE. *ge-*.]

ibouȝt, see büggen.

ibrouȝt, see bringen.

ich, *pers. pron.* 1. *sg. nom.* I, 21, 22, 39, 41 ...

if, see ȝif.

ihēren, *wk. vb.* to hear, obey ; *inf.* **ihēre,** 1, 279, 437 ; *pret. sg.* **ihērde,** 386, 457, 513 ; — *pl.* **ihērde(n),** 59, 236. Cp. hēren.

ilast, see lasten.

ilk, *adj.* same, 89, 126, 144, 216 ; **þilke** (= þe ilke), 392, 435, 479.

ilǭren, see lēsen.

in,¹ *adv.* in, 102 ; **þer ... in,** wherein, 469.

in,² *prep.* in, on (time), 19, 23, 25, 31 ... ; **þat ... in,** wherein, 95.

inǒuȝ, *adv.* enough, sufficiently, 450, 452, 485.

inǒwe, *adj. pl.* enough, 524.

intō, *prep.* into, 116, 119, 142, 145 ...

ioie, *sb.* joy, 525.

isēn, *str. vb.* V. to see ; *inf.* **isē(n),** 56, 78, 124, 154, 337 ; *pret. sg.* **isauȝ,** 471 ; — *pl.* **iseye,** 356. Cp. also sēn.

islawe, *str. vb.* VI. *p.p.* slain, 179, 307, 308, 409.

isǭld, see süllen.

isouȝt, see sēchen.

ispreind, see sprengen.

itǭld, see tellen.

iwis,¹ *sb.* certainty, assurance ; **mid iwisse,** assuredly, 56, 217, 307, 308.

iwis,² *adv.* assuredly, in truth, 172, 212, 478.

kin, see kün.

kīn, see kȳn.

king, *sb.* king, 188, 191, 193, 207 ...

kissen, see küssen.

knēlen, *wk. vb.* to kneel ; *inf.* **knēle,** 367.

knetten, *wk. vb.* to bind ; *pret. pl.* knetten, 43.

kniȝt, *sb.* knight, 151, 160, 292, 524 ...

kniȝtchīld, *sb.* knightly youth, 367.

knōwen, *str. vb. redup.* to know; *inf.* knōwe, 198; *pret. sg.* knēw, 385; *pret. subj. pl.* knēwe, 424.

kuin, see kȳn.

kün, *sb.* family, kindred, lineage, 125, 497, 532; kin, 181.

kürtel, *sb.* kirtle, coat, 99, 101, 171, 173.

küssen, *wk. vb.* to kiss; *inf.* kisse, 216, 389, 474; *pres. ind. sg.* kisseþ, 490; küsseþ, 491.

kȳn, *sb.* kine, cattle; kȳn, 287; kīn, 288, 289; kuin, 284. (Cp. § 5, 12.)

lasten, *wk. vb.* to last; *pres. ind. sg.* ilast, 460; lasteþ (future meaning), 500.

lawe, *sb.* law, 23.

lawȝen, *str. vb.* VI. to laugh; *pres. ind. pl.* lawȝeþ, 108.

lēden, *wk. vb.* (1) to lead, bring; *inf.* lēde, 119; *pres. ind. pl.* lēdeþ, 137, 142, 465; *pret. sg.* ladde, 25; — *pl.* ladden, 115, 145, 150; (2) to endure, suffer; *inf.* lēde, 183.

lēf, *adj.* dear, pleasant, agreeable, 9, 213, 226; hem is lēf = they are eager, 130; *comp.* lēuere, 6, 253, 277, 336 ... ; *super.* lēueste, 520.

lēne, *adj.* lean, thin, 286, 289, 304.

lēsen, *str. vb.* II. to lose; *pret. sg.* lēs, 433; *p.p.* ilōren, 461.

lēten, *str. vb. redup.* (1) to cease, stop; *inf.* lēte, 536; *pret. sg.* lēt, 21; (2) to let, allow; *pres. subj. pl.* lēte, 167; *pret. subj.* lette, 36; (3) to let in, *pret. subj.* (in) let, 369, note; (4) to cause,

imp. lēt, 301, 379; *pret. sg.* lette, 163, 234, 390 ...

lēue, *sb.* leave; nōmen lēue = they took leave, 404.

lēuedi, *sb.* lady, 153, 201, 203, 226.

lēuen, *wk. vb.* to grant, allow; *pres. subj. sg.* lēue, 37.

lēuen, *wk. vb.* to be left behind, to remain; *pret. sg.* lēuede, 64.

lēuere, lēueste, see lēf.

libben, *wk. vb.* to live; *inf.* libbe, 253, 277; *pret. sg.* liuede, 23, 25.

līcame, *sb.* body, 9.

līf, *sb.* life, 25, 195, 433, 460 ... ; of līue = dead, 336. See a līue.

līfdawes, *sb. pl.* days of one's life; *dat. pl.* līfdawe, 24, 309. See dai.

lift, *sb.* air, 261, 267.

lilie, *sb.* lily, 148.

liġġen, *str. vb.* V. to lie, lie (in prison); *inf.* liġġe, 12; *pres. ind.* 3. *sg.* līþ, 271, 274; — *pl.* liġġeþ, 249, 250; *pret. sg.* lai, 295.

liȝten, *wk. vb.* to alight, dismount; *pret. sg.* liȝte, 162.

liuede, see libben.

loc, *sb.* lock (of hair), 175.

lōkien, *wk. vb.* to look, see; *imp. pl.* lōkeþ (we), 90, 227; *pret. sg.* lōkede, 426.

lōnd, *sb.* land, country, 23, 25, 113, 116 ...

lōng, *adj.* long, 127, 146, 283.

lōnge, *adv.* long, 8, 244, 249, 253 ...

lōude, *adv.* loudly, 108, 224, 231.

lōue, *sb.* love, 349, 379, 520, 522.

lōuien, *wk. vb.* to love; *inf.* lōuie, 214; *pres. ind. pl.* lōuieþ, 190; *pret. sg.* lōuede, 23, 195, 433, 436 ... ; — *pl.* lōueden, 5.

lōuerd, *sb.* lord, 16, 72, 245, 298 ...

lōþ, *adj.* hateful, 9.

lōuten, *str. vb.* II. to bow down; *inf.* lōuten, 46.

lŭt, *adj.* little, slight, 273.

lŭtel, *adj.* little, small, poor, 11; *adverbially,* (a) lŭtel = a little, 81, 405.

lŭþer, *adj.* evil, 10, 180.

māden, see māken.

mai, *anom. vb* am able, can; *pres.* 1. *sg.* mai, 519, 527; — 2. *sg.* miʒt, 84, 212; —3. *sg.* mai, 52, 62, 75, 235 ...; —*pl.* mōwen, 124, 279; *pres. subj.* 1. *sg.* mōwe, 498; *pret. ind. sg.* miʒte, 104, 128, 434; — *pl.* miʒten, 17; *pret. subj. sg.* 226, 241.

maiden, *sb.* maiden, 153.

māken, *wk. vb.* to make; *inf.* māke(n), 207, 365, 440, 496; *pres. ind. sg.* mākeþ, 338, 432; *pret. pl.* māden, 331, 454.

māle, *sb.* bag, sack, 115.

man, *sb.* man, 31, 62, 76, 77 ...; *pl.* men, 5.

mani, *adj.* many (a), 147, 155, 160, 181 ...

mantel, *sb* mantle, 223, 515.

mawe, *sb* stomach, maw, 14.

me,[1] *indef. pron.* one, 36, 270, 304, 327.

mē,[2] *pers. pron.* 1. *sg. acc.* and *dat.* me, 41, 45, 46, 49 ...

mēde, *sb* meadow; *dat.* medewe, 283.

medewe, see mēde.

menestral, *sb.* minstrel, 360.

meri, see mŭri.

mēst, *adj. super.* greatest, 269, 508, 526, 538.

mester, *sb.* office, 268.

mēte, *sb.* meat, food, 14, 105, 317, 331 ..

mēten, *str. vb.* V. to measure; *inf.* mēten, 399.

mēten, *wk. vb.* to dream (*pers.* or

impers. + *dat.*); *inf.* mēte (*pers*) 255; *pret. sg.* mette (*impers.*) 35; (*pers.*) 258, 281.

mētere, *sb.* dreamer, 88.

mēting, *sb.* dreaming, dream, 40, 90.

mī, *poss. adj.* of *pers. pron.* 1. *sg.* my, 37, 42, 46, 48 ...

mid, *prep.* with, 56, 85, 107, 114 ... prŏud mid, proud of, 188; mid þefþe, in the act of theft.

miʒt(e)(n), see mai.

mīne, *poss. adj.* of *pers pron.* 1. *sg.* my, mine, 40, 42, 205.

mō, *sb.* and *adj.* more, 237, 430.

mōd, *sb.* heart, mind, 107.

mōder, *sb.* mother, 42, 57, 138, 155 ...

mōn, *sb.* lamentation, complaint, 331, 338, 432, 454.

mōne, *sb* moon, 48, 478.

mōre,[1] *quasi-sb. comp.* more, 165.

mōre,[2] *adv. comp.* more, 30, 436.

morewentīde, *sb.* morning 406.

mōst, see mōt.

mōt, *anom. vb.* must, am obliged, am able; *pres.* 1. *sg.* mōt, 536; — 2. *sg.* mōst, 69; — 3 *sg.* mōt (= is able), 534; — *pl.* mōte(n), 58, 340.

mōwe, *sb.* heap of corn, 357. [OE. *mūga.*]

mōwe(n), see mai.

mŭche(l),[1] *adj.* great, 110, 149, 155, 184 ...

mŭchel,[2] *adv.* by far, greatly, 20.

mŭri, *adj.* merry, pleasant, 255; meri, 5.

nabbeþ, nabbi, nadda, see habben.

nāked, *adj.* naked, 102.

nāle, see āle.

nāme, *sb.* name, 4; nōme, 383.

nap, *sb.* cup, bowl, 401, 412, 420, 421 ...; *pl.* nappes, 507.

nas, see bēn.

naþ, see habben.

ne, *neg.* not, 20, 38, 73, 75 ...
neb, *sb.* face, 176, 490.
nēd, *sb.* need, 58, 381 ; *adverbially*,
nēde (= of necessity, needs),
340, 536.
nei3, *adv.* near, almost, 126, 333.
neiþer ... ne, *conj.* neither ... nor,
106, 292.
nellic(h), neltóu, see wóle.
nēnde, see ēnde.
nēndinge, see ēndinge.
nęnne, *adj.* no, none, not any, 235.
nęr, *adv.* (*comp.* to nei3), nearer,
124.
nēre, see bēn.
nęuer(e), *adv.* never, 30, 174, 178,
211 ...
nēwe, *adj.* new, 246.
nextfǫlde, *adj.* used as *sb.* kindred,
intimate friends, 497 (note).
ni3t, *sb.* night, 254, 320, 322,
352 ...
nimen, *str. vb.* IV. to seize, take,
take (heed, leave) ; *inf.* nime,
225, 234 ; *pres. ind. pl.* nimeþ,
141, 465 ; *pres. subj. pl.* nime,
89 ; *imp. pl.* nimeþ, 344, 345,
350 ; *pret. sg.* nam, 273, 399,
401 ; — *pl.* nōmen, 404 ; *p.p.*
inōme, 93, 205, 410, 412 ...
nis, see bēn.
nǫ,¹ see nǫn.
nǫ,² *conj.* nor, 434 (note).
nolde, see wóle.
nǫme, see nāme.
nǫn, *adj.* no, none, not one, 19,
38, 73, 199 ... ; nǫ, 62, 136, 143,
211 ... Cp. also nęnne.
nǫt, see wǫt.
nóu,¹ *adv.* now, nowadays, 1, 6,
21, 31 ...
nóu,² *conj.* now that, since, 93.
nou3t, *sb.* naught, nothing, 3, 197 ;
adverbially, in no wise, not, 96,
215, 258, 376 ...
nóuþe, *adv.* now, 243.
nǫ wi3t, see wi3t.
nuste, see wǫt.

o, see of.²
ǭ, see ǭn.
of,¹ *adv* off, 101, 224.
of,² *prep.* (1) of, about, concerning,
with, 2, 4, 14, 22 ... ; o, 181 ;
(2) from, off, 101, 162, 416 ... ;
of līue, see līf.
oftāken, *str. vb.* VI. to overtake ;
pret. sg. oftōk, 360.
ofte, *adv.* often, 330.
ǭld, *adj.* old, 252, 276, 324, 380 ;
see ęld.
on, *prep.* on, on to, of (of sickness),
26, 27, 161, 343 ...
ǭn, *numeral*, one, a, an, 2, 4,
80, 127 ... ; ǭ, 94, 103 ; þǭnes
(= þe ǭnes), 402 ; at ǭn,
agreed, 131.
ǭnde, *sb.* hatred, envy, malice, 110.
onswerien, *wk. vb.* to answer ;
pret. sg. onswerede, 79.
óu, see 3óu.
ōþer, *adj.* other, 47, 258, 532 ; *pl.*
ōþre, 105, 241 ; ōþer, 286 ; al
an ōþer, altogether differently,
92 (note).
ōþer, *conj.* or, or else, 180.
ǭuerstī3en, *str. vb.* I. to surmount,
rise above ; *pret. sg.* ǭuerstei3,
20.
ou3te, *anom. vb.* ought ; *pres. ind.
pl* ou3te (we), 278.
óur, óure, *poss. adj.* of *pers. pron.*
1. *pl.* our, 11, 13, 43, 62 ... ;
ṽre, 72, 384.
óut, *adv* out, 7, 163, 193, 267.
óutdrawen, *str. vb.* VI. to draw
(a sword) ; *p.p.* óutdrawe, 408.
ǭwe, *adj.* own, 195.

pal, *sb.* costly cloth, 425, 517.
panes, *sb. pl.* pennies, coins, 133
(note).
paradīs, *sb.* Paradise, Eden, 200.
patriarke, *sb.* patriarch, 2, 4.
pet, *dat.* pette, *sb.* pit, 95, 102, 104,
107 ...
pīne, *sb.* suffering, 337.

pīpe, *sb.* pipe, 525.

platten, *wk. vb.* to plait ; *pret. sg.* platte, 516.

pliȝten, *wk. vb.* to pledge ; *pret. pl.* pliȝten, 446, 456.

pōre, *adj.* poor, 190, 192.

porter, *sb.* porter, gatekeeper, 369.

prēne, *sb.* pin, 402 (note).

prīs, *sb.* honour, advantage, profit, 11.

prisōn, *sb.* prison, 250, 265, 274.

próud, *adj.* proud ; próud mid, proud of, 188 ; próut, 146.

próut, see próud.

prūde, prūte, *sb.* pride, 215, 313 ; *gen. pl.* prūdene (= of all splendid things), 508.

prūte, see prūde.

pull, *sb.* pool, 18 (note).

purs, *sb.* purse, 133.

putten, *wk. vb.* to put, place ; *pret. sg.* putte, 402.

quellen, *wk. vb.* to kill, 89, 93, 111.

quēne, *sb.* queen, 195, 204, 219, 223.

quīten, *wk. vb.* to set free, release ; *pres. ind.* 1. *sg.* quīte, 303 (note).

quod, *str. vb.* V. *pret. sing.* said, 203, 204, 378.

raþer, *adv. comp.* first, before, previously, 314.

rēd, *adj.* red, 398, 415.

rēden, *str. vb. redup.* to read, advise, interpret ; *inf.* rēde(n), 184, 293, 311, 323.

rēmen, *wk. vb.* to scream, cry out ; *inf.* rēme, 224, 231.

rēnden, *wk. vb.* to tear, rend ; *inf.* rēnden, 176.

rēpen, reaped, 43. Cp. § 6, 1.

rēuful, *adj.* sad, melancholy, 30.

rēuþe, *sb.* grief, sorrow, 104, 184.

rēuþful, *adj.* mournful, 418.

rēwen, *str. vb.* II. to rue (*impers.*);

inf. rēwe, 423 ; *pres. ind.* 3. *sg.* rēweþ, 347.

riche, *adj.* rich, powerful, 112, 145, 190, 192... ; *super.* richest, 207.

rīden, *str. vb.* I. to ride ; *nf.* rīde, 167, 407 ; *pres. ind. pl.* rīdeþ, 502 ; *pret. sg.* rōd, 282, 521.

riȝt, *adv.* very, entirely, straight, (with *neg.*) at all, 15, 83, 141, 197.

riȝtwīs, *adj.* righteous, 278, 328.

ring, *sb.* ring, 507.

rīued, *adv.* plentifully, in great numbers, 18 (note).

rōp, *sb.* rope, 127.

rēwe, *sb.* row ; *adverbially,* bi rēwe, in turn, 491.

rūm, *adj.* large, 99.

rūmen, *wk. vb.* to enlarge, distend ; *inf.* rūme, 7. [OE. *rȳman.*]

sabelīn, *sb.* sable, 505.

sak, *sb.* sack, 402, 420.

sāke, *sb.* sake ; tō . . . sāke, for the sake of, 504.

sāle, *sb.* sale ; tō sāle, for sale, 116, 122.

sēchen, *wk. vb.* to seek ; *inf.* sēche(n), 70, 74 ; sēch, 341 ; *pres. ind.* 3. *sg.* sēcheþ, 75, 78 ; *pret. sg.* souȝte, 74 ; isouȝt, 420.

sēþsīde, *sb.* seaside, 529.

seġġen, siġġen, *wk. vb.* to say ; *pres. ind. sg.* seiþ, 298, 302 ; — *pl.* siġġeþ, 88 ; seġġeþ, 512 ; *pres. subj. pl.* siġġe, 361 ; *pret. sg.* seide, 39, 53, 69, 177... ; seidich (said I), 485 ; — *pl.* seiden, 124, 410.

seidich, see seġġen.

self, *adj.* (him) self ; *dat.* selue, 191.

sēli, *adj.* innocent, 271.

selken, *adj.* silken, 516.

selue, see self.

seluer, *sb.* silver, 209, 345, 507.

sēmen, *wk. vb.* to load; *inf.* sēme, 398; *p.p.* isēmed (laden), 114, 415.

sēn, *str. vb.* V. to see; *inf.* sēn, 372; *pret. sg.* sauȝ, 173, 284, 285, 423, 489; —*pl.* seien, 112; seyen, 370, 407; *pret. subj. sg.* seye, 183. Cp. isēn.

sēnden, *wk. vb.* to send; *inf.* sēnde, 329; sēnden, 504; *pret. sg.* sende, 16, 280, 453; sente, 196.

serewe, *sb.* sorrow, 106, 466, 518.

seriant, *sb.* sergeant, servant; *pl.* serians, 225.

seruen, *wk. vb.* to serve; *inf.* serue, 269; *pres. ind.* 3. *sg.* serueþ, 191, 270; *p.p.* iserued, 392, 479.

sēstrōnd, *sb.* seashore, 140.

setten, *wk. vb.* to set, place upright; *pret. pl.* setten, 44.

seþþe(n), *adv.* and *conj.* afterwards, since, 12, 166, 327, 397 ...

seue, *numeral*, seven, 284, 286, 287, 288 ...

sibbe, *adj.* related, akin, 252, 276.

siȝȝen, see seȝȝen.

siker, *adj.* sure, secure; siker māken, to give security for, 440.

singen, *str. vb.* III. to sing; *inf.* singe, 30, 395, 527; *pres. part* singinde, 521; *pret. pl.* sungen, 396.

sinne, *sb.* sin, 182. Cp. § 7.

sīr(e), *form of address*, Sir, Sire, 266, 268, 318.

sitten, *str. vb.* V. to sit; *inf.* sitte(n), 8, 371; *pres. ind.* 3. *sg.* sit, 31, 65, 67, 107 ...; —*pl.* sitteþ, 105; *imp.* sitte ȝe, 376; *pret. pl.* sēten, 262.

skarlet, *sb.* scarlet material, 505.

skēre, *adj.* free, unhindered, 438.

slēpen, *wk. vb.* (orig. *redup.*) to

sleep; *inf.* slēpe, 12, 254; *pret. sg.* slepte, 41, 282.

smal, *adj.* small, 330.

smoc, *sb.* garment, 176.

sō,[1] *adv.* so, in the same manner, to the same degree, 19, 24, 37, 134 ...

sō,[2] *conj.* as, so, whilst, when, 22, 43 (note), 148, 395, 396; sō sōne sō, *conj.* as soon as, 161.

sōne, *sb.* son, 26, 32, 33, 37 ...

sōne, *adv.* soon, 66, 69, 131, 157 ...

sōng, *sb.* song, 5, 30, 251, 270 ...

sōr, *sb.* sorrow, pain, 518.

sōre, *adv.* sorely, 144, 389, 423, 474 ...

sōri, *adj.* sorrowful, 107, 132, 136, 172 ...

sōrimōd, *adj.* sad at heart, 174.

sōrinesse, *sb.* sorrow, grief, 183.

sōule, *sb.* soul, 9.

spēche, *sb.* speech, language, 143, 324.

spēken, *str. vb.* V. to speak; *inf.* spēke(n), 34, 37, 128, 168 ...; *pret. sg.* spac, 79, 94, 97, 117 ...

spel, *sb.* tale, 40.

spīce, *sb.* spice, 115.

sprenȝen, *wk. vb.* to besprinkle, bespatter; *p.p.* ispreind, 173.

springen, *str. vb.* III. to come, be brought (of news); *pret. sg.* sprōng, 157.

ssāken, *str. vb.* VI. to shake; *pret. sg.* ssōk, 426.

ssal, *anom. vb.* am about to, shall, have to; *pres. ind.* I. *sg.* ssal, 307, 308, 462; — 2. *sg.* ssalt, 208, 210, 266, 268 ...; — 3. *sg.* ssal, 90, 110, 211 ...; — *pl.* ssule(n), 56, 186, 265, 440 ...; *pret. sg.* and *pl.* ssolde, 87, 311, 416.

ssāme, see ssōme.

ssēf, *sb.* sheaf; *pl.* ssēues, 43, 45.

ssēnden, *wk. vb.* to disgrace; *pres. subj. pl.* ssēnde (we), 96.

sséten, *str. vb.* II. to shoot; *inf.* ssête, 194.

ssēues, see ssēf.

ssēwen, *wk. vb.* to set forth, expound; *pret. pl.* ssēweden, 121.

ssilden, *wk. vb.* shield, protect; *pres. subj. sg.* 167.

ssolde, see ssal.

ssōme, *sb.* shame, disgrace, 229, 232, 328; ssáme, 326.

ssroud, *sb.* clothes, covering, 187.

ssrüden, *wk. vb.* to clothe; *pres. ind. sg.* ssrūdeþ, 187.

ssule(n), see ssal.

stēde, *sb.* place, spot, 243. (Cp. § 5, 7.)

stēde, *sb.* steed, horse, 162, 166.

sterre, *sb.* star; *pl.* sterren, 50, 476.

stille, *adv.* quietly, in secret, 220, 228.

stīward, *sb.* steward, 158, 159, 161, 411 ...

stǫnden, *str. vb.* VI. to stand; *pret. sg.* stōd, 81, 95, 259; — *pl.* stōden, 45.

stōr, *sb.* incense, 115.

strēng, *sb.* string, 516.

strēte, *sb.* street, 146, 152, 154.

strǫng, *adj.* strong, severe, 145, 499.

strǫnge, *adv.* heavily, gravely, 247, 248.

strüpen, *wk. vb.* to strip; *pret. pl.* strüpten, 101 (note). Cp. § 5, 10.

süch,¹ *adj.* such, 328. Cp. § 7, β.

süch,² *conj.* as, as if (with *subj.*), 12 (note), 371, 382, 521.

süllen, *wk. vb.* to sell, offer (for sale); *inf.* süllen, 116, 118, 150, 379; cp. § 7, β; *p.p.* isǫld, 134.

summe, *adj.* : *pl.* some ; 180, 237.

süngen (on), *wk. vb.* to sin against; *inf.* süngen, 486.

sunne, *sb.* sun, 48, 478.

swefne, see sweuen.

swērd, *sb.* sword, 408.

swēre, *sb.* neck, 101.

swēren, *str. vb.* VI. to swear;

pret. sg. swōr, 334; —*pl.* swōre, 435; *p.p.* iswōren, 86.

swēte, *adj.* sweet, 199, 315, 533, 535.

sweuen(e), *sb.* dream, 51, 120, 263, 264 ... ; swefne, 35, 54, 55.

swikedōm, *sb.* treachery, deception, 427.

swink, *sb.* toil, hardship, 358.

swinken, *str. vb.* III. to toil; *inf.* swinke, 342.

swīþe, *adv.* very, sorely, eagerly, much, 1, 18, 34, 36.

swōwen, *str. vb. redup.* to swoon; *p.p.* iswōwe (in a swoon), 175, 458, 466.

tāken, *str. vb.* VI. to take; *pret. sg.* tōc, 517.

tāle, *sb.* story, tale, speech, 5, 28, 29, 97 ...

te, see þe.

tēld, *sb.* tent, 70.

tellen, *wk. vb.* (1) to tell; *inf.* telle(n), 3, 22, 36, 39 ... ; *pres. ind.* I. *sg.* telli (I tell), 49; telle, 51; — *pl.* telleþ, 456; *imp. pl.* telleþ, 377; *pret. sg.* tǫlde, 35, 232, 290; —*pl.* tǫlden, 263; (2) to count; *p.p.* itǫld, 133.

ten, see þen.

tēn,¹ *numeral*, ten, 26, 61, 86, 170 ...

tēn,² *str. vb.* II. to go, proceed; *inf.* tē, 77.

tēne, *sb.* trouble, anxiety, 403.

tēren, *str. vb.* IV. to tear; *pret. sg.* tar, 175.

tērnde, see þe and ērnde.

tīden, *wk. vb.* to betide, happen, *pres. subj.* 54, 55, 245.

tīding, *sb.* news, tidings, 71, 157, 206, 439 ...

tīme, *sb.* time, 488.

tis, see þis.

tō,¹ *adv.* too, 460, 500.

tō,² *prep.* to, towards, to (with *inf.*), 6, 11, 28, 29 ... ; (of time),

about, 246 ; tō . . . sāke (for
sake of), 504.

tōbrēken, *str. vb.* IV. to break
(commandment or promise);
inf. tōbrēke, 221 ; *pres. subj. sg.*
tōbrēke, 38.

tōdrawen, *str. vb.* VI. to tear to
pieces ; *p.p.* tōdrawe, 180.

tōfōre, *prep.* before, in presence
of, 191, 375, 411, 419 ...

tōȝeines, *prep.* towards, 286.

tōme, *adj.* tame, 355.

tōniȝt, *adv.* to-night, 365, 367.

tōtēren, *str. vb.* IV. to tear to
pieces ; *inf.* tōtēre, 261.

tóu, see þóu.

tōward, *prep.* towards, 87, 405.

trōuþe, *sb.* truth, faith, 221, 446,
456, 463.

trukien, *wk. vb.* (*impers.* + *dat.*)
to fail, lack ; *pret. sg.* trukede,
393, 480.

turnen, *wk. vb.* to turn ; *pres. ind.*
pl. turneþ, 417.

tūbrüǧǧe, *sb.* drawbridge, 363
(note).

twei, tweye, *numeral,* two, 27, 112.

twōlf, *numeral,* twelve, 407
(note) ; twōlue, 532.

twō, *numeral,* two, 499.

þan, þen, *conj.* than (after comparative) ; þan, 436 ; þən, 28, 165,
253, 277 ...

þane, þene, *def. art. acc. sg. masc.*
the, that ; þane, 436 ; þene, 301,
425. Cp. þen.[1]

þar(e), *adv.* there, 356, 359, 364.

þarf, darf, *anom. vb.* 3. *sg.*
(he) needs, requires ; darf, 136
(note).

þat,[1] *def. art. neut.* the, 66, 67, 77,
79 ...

þat,[2] *conj.* that, until that, so that,
17, 38, 41 ...

þat,[3] *rel. pron.* who, which, that,
that which, 20, 35, 62, 64, 72 ... ;
þat .. in, wherein, 95.

þau, see þauȝ.

þauȝ, þau, notwithstanding, although, 472 ; þau, 61.

þe,[1] *adv.* with *comparative,* the,
289.

þe, te,[2] *def. art.* the ; þe, 7, 9, 31,
34 ... ; þōnes (= þe ōnes),
402 ; atte (= at þe), 94, 104,
111, 117 ; te, 48 ; tērnde (= þe
ērnde), 87. Cp. þen, þane, þat.

þēf, *sb.* thief, scoundrel, 227 ; *pl.*
þēues, 410.

þefþe, *sb.* theft ; mid þefþe,
in the act of theft, 413.

þei, *pers. pron.* 3. *pl. nom.* they,
15, 46, 115, 262, 455.

þeiȝ, *conj.* although, 220, 233.

þen,[1] *def. art. acc.* and *dat.* the ;
acc. þen ēnde, 298, 302 ; *dat.*
þe nāle, 6 ; þə nēndinge, 29 ;
atte nēnde, 327. Cp. þane
and § 11, iv.

þen,[2] *conj.* see þan.

þenchen, *wk. vb.* to think ; *pres.*
ind. 1. *sg.* þenche, 325 ; — 3. *sg.*
þencheþ, 320, 322 ; — *p .*
þencheþ, 92, 106 ; *pret. sg.*
þouȝte, 73, 295.

þene, see þane.

þenne,[1] *adv.* then, 53, 76, 112,
382 ...

þenne,[2] *adv.* thence, 103.

þēr,[1] *adv.* there, 8, 19, 213, 225 ...

þēr,[2] *conj.* where, when, 21, 45,
199 ... ; þēr .. in, wherein, 469.

þērafter, *adv.* thereafter, after that,
90.

þērfōre, *adv.* therefore, on this
account, 59, 61, 75, 236 ...

þērinne, *adv.* thereinto, into this,
96.

þērof, *adv.* therefrom, 403.

þēse, *demons. pl.* these, 218, 337,
374, 409, 417. Cp § 11, v.

þēron, *adv.* thereon, 318.

þēstri, *adj.* dark, gloomy, 243.
[OE. þēostriȝ.]

þēues, see þēf.

þí, see þín.
þider, *adv.* thither, 8, 151, 159, 181 ..
þiderward, *adv.* thitherwards, 85.
þilk, see ilk.
þín(e), *poss. adj.* of *pers. pron.* 2. *sg.* thy, thine; þín, 217, 267, 319; þíne, 57, 58, 70, 71, 211, 299; þí, 52, 54, 55, 57 ...
þing, *sb.* thing, matter, 143, 197, 199, 212 ...; *adverbial* nọ þing, in no wise, 218.
þinkeþ, see þúnchen.
þis,*demons.* this, these, cp. § 11, v; *sg.* þis, 3, 28, 51, 95 ...; tis, 20; *pl.* 63, 105, 121 ...
þisse(n), *demons. dat. sg.* this, 197, 293, 294, 341; cp. § 11, v.
þọ,¹ *adv.* then, 17, 81, 104, 295 ...
þọ,² *conj.* when, 172, 173, 288, 294 ...
þọlede, see þọlien.
þọlien, *wk. vb.* to endure, suffer; *inf.* þọlie, 443; *pret. sg.* þọlede, 326, 328.
þọnes, see ọn.
þonken, *wk. vb.* (+ *dat. pers. acc. rei*) to give thanks; *pres. ind.* 1. *sg.* þonke, 306, 475; — 3. *sg.* þonkeþ, 245.
þóu, *pers. pron.* 2. *sg. nom.* thou, 42, 69, 82, 83 ...; þú, 82, 83, 84, 212; tóu, 38.
þouȝt, *sb.* thought, 198.
þridde, *numeral,* third, 49, 265.
þú, see þóu.
þúnchen, þinken, *wk. vb.* to seem; (1)*impers.* + *dat.*: *pres. ind. sg.* þinkeþ, 108; þúncheþ, 329, 362, 519; *pres. subj. sg.* þúnche, 233; *pret. sg.* þuȝte, 41, 45, 47, 49 ...; (2) *pers.*: *pres. ind. pl.* þúncheþ, 366.
þurȝ, *adv.* and *prep.* through, by means of, 150, 281, 315.
þus, *adv.* thus, so, 13, 79, 110.

vnderfọngen, *str. vb. redup.* to receive; *inf.* vnderfọnge, 268, 526.
vnderstọnder, *str. vb.* VI. to understand; *pres. ina.* 1. *sg.* vnderstọnde, 84.
vnfẹld, see vnfọlden.
vnfọlden, *str.vb. redup.*to unfold; *pret. sg.* vnfúld, 162 (cp. § 5, 9); vnfẹld, 222.
unfúld, see unfọlden.
vnirúde, *adj.* huge, tremendous, 20. [OE. *ungerýde.*]
vnlóuken,*str. vb.* II. to open; *inf.* vnlóuke, 163.
vp, *adv.* up, 111, 127, 376.
vpon, *prep.* upon, on to, 140.
vpriȝt, *adv.* upright, 44.
v̄re, see óur.
vs, *pers. pron.* 1. *pl. acc.* and *dat.* us, 71, 341, 345, 379, 436.
vte, *exclamation* (with *infin.*) let us; vte spẹken, 168. [OE. *uton.*]
v̆cchen, *wk. vb.* to increase, widen, . Cp. § 5, 10.
v̆rl, *sb.* earl, 291. Cp. § 5, 4.

vader, see fader.
valleþ, see fallen.
vinger, see finger.
vrom, see from.

wai, *sb.* way, 350, 406; way, 404.
was, see bẹn.
wat, see what.
water, *sb.* water, 315, 355, 390.
way, see wai.
wẹ, *pers. pron.* 1. *pl. nom.* we, 10, 41, 43, 44 ...
wel, *adv.* much, very, well, 6, 44, 68, 100 ...
welcòme, *adj.* welcome, 204.
wẹle, *sb.* happiness, prosperity, 531.
wen, see whenne.
wẹnden, *wk. vb.* to go, wend;

inf. wēnde, 69, 325, 340 ; wēnden, 404; *pres. ind. pl.* wēndeþ,
63 ; *imp. pl.* wēndeþ, 350 ; *pret.
sg.* wende, 223 ; *p.p.* iwent,
193.

wēnen, *wk. vb.* to think, deem,
hope ; *pres. ind.* 1. *sg.* wēne,
56 ; *pret. sg.* wēnde, 74, 228 ;
— *pl.* wēnden, 409 ; *pret. subj.
pl.* wēnden (if they had thought),
372.

wēp, *sb.* lamentation, weeping,
418.

wēpen,[1] *sb.* weapon ; *pl.* wēpnen,
350.

wēpen,[2] *wk. vb.* (orig. *redupl.*),
to weep ; *inf.* wēpe, 423, 489 ;
pres. ind. 3. *sg.* wēpeþ, 137,
388 ... ; *pret. sg.* wepte, 144.

wēr,[1] *adv.* whether, 136.

wēr,[2] see whēr.

wēre(n), see bēn.

wērne (= werned (?), *adj.* refused,
withheld, denied, 215 (note).

wēte, see whēte.

wey, *exclamation*, woe, alas, 110.

what, *interrog. pron. neut.* what,
52, 321 ; wat, 54, 55, 68, 90,
203 ...

when, see whenne.

whenne, *conj.* when ; when, 443;
wenne, 325, 328 ; wen, 270,
464.

whennes, *adv.* whence, 361.

whēr, *adv.* where, 459 ; wēr, 70,
123.

whēte, *sb.* wheat ; wēte, 398.

whī, *adv.* why, 459.

whider, *adv.* whither ; wòder,
77. Cp. § 5, 13.

whīle,[1] *adv.* long ago, formerly,
5.

whīle,[2] *sb.* time, while, 128.

whīt, *adj.* white, bright, 148, 222 ;
wīt, 391.

whōsō, *indef. pron.* whosoever,
29 ; wōsō, 183.

wīd, *adj.* wide, 99, 146, 530.

wīf, *sb.* wife, 26, 434 ; *dat.* wīue,
326.

wiȝt, *sb.* thing ; nō wiȝt, nothing,
323, 393, 480.

wīlde, *adj.* wild, 355, 522.

wille, *sb.* (1) will, 52, 68, 85,
203 ... ; wil, 210 ; (2) as much
as one can wish for, wil, 208.

wimman, *sb.* woman, 198, 199.

wimpel, *sb.* wimple, 224.

wīn, *sb.* wine, 28, 257, 394, 445 ...

wīnȝard, *sb.* vineyard, 256.

winne, *sb.* joy, pleasure, 531. Cp.
§ 5, 7.

winnen, *str. vb.* III. to gain, win,
beget ; *pret. sg.* wan, 26, 27 ;
p.p. iwònne, 477.

wīpen, *wk. vb.* to wipe ; *inf.* wīpe,
490.

wīs, *adj.* wise, 123, 129, 324.

wīse, *sb.* wise, manner, 219, 221,
424.

wīt, see whīt.

witen, *wk. vb.* to guard, keep ;
inf. witen, 63.

wīue, see wīf.

wiþ, *prep.* with, 173, 196, 369,
516, 517.

wiþinne, *prep.* inside, within, 402.

wō,[1] *adj.* sorrowful, 236, 238.

wō,[2] *sb.* woe, calamity, 244, 533;
hem was wō, 59; him was
wō, 75 ; wō is mē, 177.

wōd, *adj.* mad, raving, 15.

wòde, *sb.* wood, 194, 230.

wòder, see whider.

wòle, *anom. vb.* I will, mean to ;
pres. ind. 1. *sg.* wòle, 21, 39,
206 ... ; wòlle, 439 ; — 2. *sg.*
wòlt, 82, 83 ; — 3. *sg.* wòle, 54,
55, 62 ... ; — *pl.* wòlleþ, 93, 111,
119 ... ; wòlle ȝe (we), 1, 118,
437 ; *pret. sg.* wolde, 77, 78,
260 ; — *pl.* wolde, 508.   With
negation : *pres. ind.* 1. *sg.* nellic, 3 ; nellich, 463 ; — 2. *sg.*
neltóu, 459 ; *pret. sg.* nolde,
219, 221, 424.

wǫmbe, *sb.* belly, 7, 11.

wǒnder, *sb.* wonder, surprise; **hem þuȝte wǒnder**, they marvelled, 155; **þunche hit no wǒnder**, let it seem no marvel, 233.

wǒnderþing, *sb.* a wonderful or curious thing, 400.

wondrien, *wk. vb.* to wander; *pres. part.* **wondrinde**, 76.

wǫne, *sb.* scarcity, lack, 317, 331.

wǫp, *sb.* weeping, lamentation, 128.

wǒrd, *sb.* word, story, tale, report, 1, 38, 126, 192 ...

wǒrld, *sb.* world, 19.

wǒrpen, *str. vb.* III. to cast, throw; *imp.* **wǒrpeþ**, 96; *pret. pl.* **worpen**, 102.

wǒrssipe, *sb.* honour, dignity, 269, 526, 538.

wǒrse, *adj. comp.* worse, 537.

wǒrþen ,*str. vb.* III. to be, become; *pres. ind.* 3. *sg.* **wǒrþ**, 120; — *pl.* **wǒrþeþ**, 414; *pres. subj. sg.* **wǒrþe**, 427.

wǫt, *anom. vb.* I know; *pres. ind.* 1. *sg.* **wǫt**, 307, 308; — 3. *sg.* **wǫt**, 47. With negation: *pres. ind.* 3. *sg.* **nǫt**, 238, 321; *pret.* 3. *sg.* **nüste**, 197.

wǒuȝ, *sb.* wrong, evil; **wǒuȝ hadden**, ye did wrong, 486.

wrecched, *adj.* wretched, 460.

wreyen, *wk. vb.* to accuse; *p.p.* **iwreyed**, 247, 248.

wringen, *str. vb.* III. to wring (the hands), to press (wine from grapes); *inf.* **wringe**, 458; *pres. ind.* 3. *sg.* **wringeþ**, 109, 185; — *pl.* **wringeþ**, 422; *pret. sg.* **wrǎng**, 132; **wrǫng**, 257, 335.

wrǫng, *sb.* injustice; *adverbially*, **mid wrǫnge**, unjustly, 250, 271, 274.